Norman Maclean

The Confluence American Authors Series
James R. Hepworth, Series Editor
Lewis Clark State College

TCAAS 2

AMERICAN AUTHORS SERIES

Norman Maclean

edited by

Ron McFarland and Hugh Nichols

Confluence Press, Inc.   Lewiston, Idaho

Publication of this book is made possible by grants from The Idaho Commis-
sion on the Arts, a state agency, and the National Endowment for the Arts in
Washington, D.C., a federal agency.

Second Printing

Published by
  Confluence Press, Inc.
8th Avenue & 6th Street
Lewiston, Idaho 83501

Distributed to the trade by
National Book Network
4720-A Boston Way
Lanham, Maryland 20706

About the Series

The aim of this series is to present the best in contemporary critical opinion on modern and contemporary American authors alongside interviews, excerpts, bibliographies, letters, photographs, and manuscript selections. In some cases, however, as in Nancy Colberg's forthcoming descriptive bibliography of Wallace Stegner, we may limit a particular volume to one critical task. Regardless, our purpose for publishing each volume remains essentially the same: to make a real and lasting contribution to American literary studies. We hope to focus attention on modern and contemporary American authors whose work merits close examination, but especially upon those writers, like Norman Maclean, whose work recognizes that in *being* American our literature is intimately connected with a place. And that *that* place is a story that has already happened many times and is continuing to happen.

This volume on Norman Maclean is the first collection of his miscellaneous writing, but it by no means collects all of it. Likewise, our gathering of critical articles about Maclean's fiction, several of them commissioned especially for this volume, is the first collection of criticism that we know of ever published on Maclean's *A River*

Runs Through It and Other Stories. We hope and trust that it will not be the last.

James R. Hepworth, Series Editor

Table of Contents

Norman Maclean

Introduction

The story of Norman Maclean and his "little book" are now legend: how the author, at 73 and retired after a long and distinguished teaching career at the University of Chicago, had written and published a slender collection composed of a title novella, "A River Runs Through It," a short story, "Logging and Pimping and 'Your Pal, Jim,' " and a second novella, "USFS 1919: The Ranger, the Cook, and a Hole in the Sky"; how the manuscript was rejected by three commercial publishing houses (including Alfred A. Knopf) before it was taken by the University of Chicago Press in an unprecedented first (and only) venture into fiction; how the book was widely and enthusiastically reviewed—a "stunning debut," said *Publishers Weekly*; how it narrowly missed the 1977 Pulitzer Prize for fiction when the Advisory Board refused to accept the jury's recommendation on the grounds that it was a "lean" year in fiction; and how to date the book has sold in excess of 160,000 copies and, according to Allen Fitchen, the former editor at Chicago, almost entirely "through word of mouth—a phenomenon prayed for by every advertising and promotion manager in the business."

All reasons enough, the editors believe, for a book about a book.

The "phenomenon" of Norman Maclean and his single volume of fiction suggest to us the presence of more complex and enduring qualities, qualities reflected by America's major works of fiction. Not surprisingly, the additional essays, stories, and interviews by and about Maclean that we have collected in this volume lend confirmation to such a conclusion.

We have not represented Maclean's contributions to literary scholarship here. They consist of just two essays, both published in Ronald S. Crane's *Critics and Criticism* (1952) and both of substantial depth and quality. Instead, we have collected the scattered essays and stories that constitute the remainder of his published writing, and we have added four essays drawn from lectures given between 1977 and 1987. "The Hidden Art of a Good Story" elucidates Maclean's most recent views about the artistry of his own fiction. He delivered this talk in the spring of 1987 at the annual Wallace Stegner Lecture at Lewis Clark State College in Lewiston, Idaho. "Montana Memory" (1977) was given at the Institute of the Rockies in Billings, Montana. It explores the intertwining relationships between history and story telling and between "Montana Life" and "life itself." In "Teaching and Story Telling" (a 1978 talk given at both the University of Chicago and Montana State University in Bozeman), Maclean comes close to stating his own "poetics": "What could be wrong with hoping to make something beautiful, true, and good?" And in "A Man I Met in Mann Gulch," Maclean grants us a glimpse at the subject of his most recent manuscript, the Mann Gulch fire of 1949. The latter lecture was given in 1979 to the Intermountain Fire Research Council at Missoula.

In a recent interview Maclean described his piece on physicist Albert Michelson, " 'Billiards is a Good Game': Gamesmanship and America's First Nobel Prize Scientist," as "one of the best things I ever wrote." We are pleased to reprint this work from the *University of Chicago Magazine*, along with " 'This Quarter I Am Taking McKeon': A Few Remarks on the Art of Teaching." Maclean received three awards for excellence in undergraduate teaching during his 45 years at the University of Chicago. We have also included a brief autobiographical sketch, which Maclean prepared for Studs Terkel's *American Dreams*, and we have reprinted two essays on writing, "The Pure and the Good: On Baseball and Backpacking," from the *Association of Departments of English Bulletin*, and "The Woods, Books, and Truant Officers," from *Chicago* magazine. We especially enjoyed Maclean's story, "Retrievers Good and Bad," from *Esquire*, and we believe readers will recognize in it the voice from his better known fiction.

We believe these additional stories and essays contribute significantly to Norman Maclean's canon. We have proceeded from the assumption that most readers are already familiar with the stories in *A River Runs Through It and Other Stories*. Accordingly, rather than reprint selections from that volume, we have chosen to bring together material by our author that is less accessible.

The two interviews neatly complement Maclean's own biographical sketch, "Generations: First and Second," thus enlarging a necessary biographical dimension in the collection. They attest to the curiosity, not only about a man who begins a second career after age 70, but also about a University of Chicago English professor who is part fly fisherman, lumberjack, forest service fire-fighter, and general hell-raiser. William Kittredge and Annick Smith's extended interview constitutes a small autobiography. Pete Dexter's interview, published in *Esquire* in 1981, records his conversations with Maclean during a visit to his summer hermitage at Seeley Lake, Montana.

Among the essays in appreciation and criticism, we are pleased to offer four new and original examinations of Maclean's fiction solicited just for this volume. Wallace Stegner's "Haunted by Waters" judiciously puzzles over the "astonishing success" of Maclean's "little book," in light of its almost systematic violation of *all* of the "orthodoxies of the contemporary short story form." Wendell Berry's "Style and Grace" probes the differences in the concept of tragedy revealed by Maclean's title novella and Hemingway's "Big Two-Hearted River." In "Mo-nah-se-tah, the Whore, and Three Scottish Women," Mary Blew explores how Maclean's female characters relate the tradition of light and dark women in

American fiction. And Glen Love, taking his cue from Maclean's own statement that "scholars" are *one* intended audience for his stories, discovers informing "undercurrents" of the fiction in the author's scholarly work on lyric poetry.

To this same section, we have added reprints of three essays focusing more exclusively upon the novella, "A River Runs Through It": Harold Simonson's seminal analysis of the work's theological theme; Walter Hesford's study of its relationship to the tradition of "piscatory prose" exemplified by Isaac Walton and Henry Thoreau; and Gordon Brittan, Jr.'s Montana State University Honors Lecture viewing the novella from the perspective of Western Regionalism. A convenient chronology and annotated bibliography round out our collection, for those who wish further acquaintance with Maclean's prose. Throughout, we have permitted ourselves only minor editing changes (. . .) and deletions (***), the latter most typically involving certain recurring anecdotes or discussions of the closing section of "A River Runs Through It."

Certainly we are indebted most centrally for this volume to Norman Maclean himself. He not only created an American "classic" for our pleasure, but he also gave us invaluable help in bringing this book-about-a-book to fruition. Our gratitude as well to Norman's daughter, Jean, his son, John, and Jean's husband, Joel Snyder, all of whom provided essential assistance throughout the project. We are particularly indebted to Jean for her efforts in locating the photographs which grace the book. And finally, our thanks to Vana Wrigley for her indispensable work on the manuscript; and to Jim Hepworth, the publisher at Confluence Press, who was the genesis of it all.

Ron McFarland
Hugh O. Nichols

Chronology

1902   born Norman Fitzroy Maclean in Clarinda, Iowa, on 23 December to John Norman and Clara (Davidson) Maclean—father a Presbyterian minister

1909   family (including brother, Paul, three years younger) moves to Missoula, Montana; Norman Maclean is tutored by his father in religion, literature, and fly fishing

1913   enters public schools

1917   begins working summers for the U. S. Forest Service

1920   enrolls at Dartmouth College in Hanover, New Hampshire

1922   builds cabin at Seeley Lake, Montana with his father; has returned most summers ever since

1924   receives A.B. from Dartmouth College

1924–26   teaches as a teaching assistant at Dartmouth

1926–28   returns to Montana to work for the Forest Service; meets Jessie Burns at a Christmas party

1928   moves to the University of Chicago as a graduate assistant in English, returning to Montana during summers

1931   promoted to instructor; marries Jessie Burns, his father performing the ceremony, on 24 September

1932   receives first Quantrell Award for Excellence in Undergraduate Teaching at the University of Chicago

1938   brother Paul, a newspaperman, is murdered in Chicago

1940   receives second Quantrell Award for Excellence in Undergraduate Teaching at Chicago; receives Ph.D. from University of Chicago

1942–45   serves as dean of students at Chicago

1942   daughter, Jean Burns, born in Chicago on 26 January; serves as acting director for Institute on Military Studies (1943-45); co-author (with Everett C. Olson) of *Manual of Instruction in Military Maps and Aerial Photographs*

1943   son, John Norman, born in Chicago on 10 May

1949   Mann Gulch fire near Helena, death of 13 smoke jumpers (subject of work in progress)

1952   two scholarly essays published in *Critics and Criti-*

cism(University of Chicago Press), edited by Ronald S. Crane: "Episode, Scene, Speech, and Word: The Madness of Lear" and "From Action to Image: Theories of the Lyric in the Eighteenth Century"; 1952–66, chairman of the Committee on General Studies in the Humanities

1962–72   William Rainey Harper Professor of English Literature

1968   wife Jessie dies

1973   retires from teaching at the University of Chicago; receives third Quantrell Award for Excellence in Undergraduate Teaching

1974   " 'This Quarter I Am Taking McKeon': A Few Remarks on the Art of Teaching," address published as an essay in *University of Chicago Magazine*

1975   " 'Billiards is a Good Game': Gamesmanship and America's First Nobel Prize Scientist," essay published in *University of Chicago Magazine*

1976   *A River Runs Through It and Other Stories* published by University of Chicago Press; nominated for Pulitzer Prize

1977   "Retrievers Good and Bad," essay in *Esquire*

1977   "The Woods, Books, and Truant Officers," essay published in *Chicago* magazine

1979   "The Pure and the Good: On Baseball and Backpacking," essay in *Association of Departments of English Bulletin*

1980   receives honorary Litt. D. from Montana State University

1981   receives honorary Litt. D. from the University of Montana

1987   delivers Wallace Stegner Lecture at Lewis Clark State College, Lewiston, Idaho

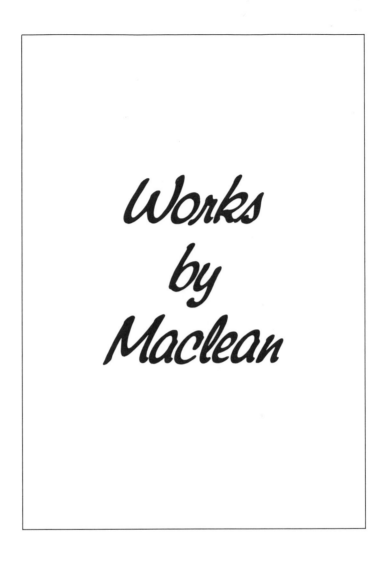

Works
by
Maclean

Generations:
First and Second

Norman Maclean*

My father and mother were immigrants from Canada. My father was all Scotch and came from Nova Scotia, from a large family that was on poor land. His great belief was in all men being equal under God. That old Bobby Burns line: A man's a man for a' that and a' that. He was a Presbyterian minister, and it was very deep with him.

My father loved America so much that, although he had a rather heavy Scotch burr when he came to this country, by the time I was born, it was all gone. He regarded it as his American duty to get rid of it. He despised Scotch Presbyterian ministers who went heavy on their Scotch burr. He put a terrific commitment on me to be an American. I, the eldest son, was expected to complete the job.

He told me I had to learn the American language. He spoke beautifully, but he didn't have the American idioms. He kept me home until I was ten and a half to teach me. He taught me how to write American. No courses in show-and-tell and personality ad-

*"Generations: First and Second" is reprinted from *American Dreams: Lost and Found* by Studs Terkel (1980), pp. 112-114, published by Pantheon Books. Copyright © 1980 by Pantheon Books, a division of Random House, Inc. Reprinted by permission of the publisher.

justment. (Laughs.) I was young and I thought I was tough and I
knew it was beautiful and I was a little bit crazy but hadn't noticed
it yet. You took those little pieces of American speech and listened
carefully for 'em and you put them together. My American training
went clear down into my language.

He was great on rhythm. He read us the Bible every morning.
We got down on our knees by our chairs and we prayed. We had
it twice a day, the great King James translation, after breakfast and
after what we called supper.

Literature was important to him: the prose of Mark Twain, and
the odd combination of Franklin Roosevelt and Wilson and Whitman. He knew it wasn't English. It was American. He couldn't get
over the fact that Wilson was the son of a Presbyterian minister.
He was the model for many generations of prose writers, including
Roosevelt.

The family was the center of the universe and the center of America. I don't know if we have *an* American Dream. We have American Dreams. One of his biggest dreams was the dream of great
education in this country and the necessity of every person to be
educated.

I was the first person in his family not to make his living with his
hands. "Maclean" means son of a carpenter. That's what my family had been. They were all carpenters. My father was the pride
and joy of his sisters because he made his living without his hands.
He was a marvelous carpenter himself. He and I, way back in 1921,
made this log cabin out there that's still mine.

Working with hands is one of our deepest and most beautiful
characteristics. I think the most beautiful parts of the human body
are the hands of certain men and women. I can't keep my eyes off
them. I was brought up to believe that hands were the instrument
of the mind. Even doing simple things. I still look pretty good with
an axe. My father was very stylish with any tool he worked with.
Yeah, the fishing rod also. He was just beautiful, pick up a four-
ounce rod and throw that line across the Blackfoot River. It was
just something beautiful to behold.

Roughly, I've managed one way or another till now to continue a life that is half intellectual and half back in the woods. I kept my cabin out there, although my family died long ago. Now that I'm retired, I spend a third of my life out there. I stay as long as the weather permits me. October, until the elk season is over.

In the city I cultivate beauty of several kinds. In twenty minutes, I can be where there are beaver and deer. I go walking practically every afternoon. Three or four times a week, I go out into the country. I've learned another kind of beauty we didn't have. I think the industrial geometric beauty of Chicago is just beyond belief. To go up the Calumet River by boat and see all those big elevators and cranes and all the big stuff over that dirty river, this is just pure design. Cezanne couldn't find more beautiful geometrical patterns. If I had to name the number one most beautiful sight in the world, given my taste, I would say standing at night by the Planetarium, looking across the bay at the big Hancock and Sears buildings. No place more beautiful. You can't be provincial about beauty.

As I've grown older, I've tried to put together the dreams into my own life. My cabin is only sixteen miles from the glaciers. It snows every month out there. And there are the Gothic halls of the University of Chicago. If you know of a more beautiful city college in the world, architecturally, I'd like to know it. University of London, Oxford, they're just outhouses in comparison.

You have to be gifted with a long life to attain a dream and make it harmonious. I feel infinitely grateful in my old age that I've had in this country, within my family, the training needed to be the best that was in me. It's no great thing, but at seventy-five, I'm fulfilled. There aren't any big pieces in me that never got a chance to come out. They may say at the end of my life, I have no alibis. I have two children of my own, whom I admire and love and try not to annoy very much. I see my father going right on with my children. You've got to pass the ball along.

Retrievers
Good and Bad

Norman Maclean*

The day I was born, as I was to be often told, my father gave me a dog for a birthday present. Very early in life, then, I was to learn about the power of odd coincidence, because my dog turned out to be a duck dog and my father turned out to be a duck hunter and evidently, at least in my infancy, I did not resemble a duck and the dog did not give a damn about me. We talk painfully about father and mother rejections, but if you are going in for rejections, there is nothing like being the supposed infant owner of an animal and wanting to be loved by it and instead being studied by yellow eyes that wished you were a dead duck. Even so, in many ways and for long periods of the year, the dog belonged more to my mother than to my father or to me.

My father was a Scotch Presbyterian minister. He was intellectual and somewhat poetical and referred to Methodists as Baptists who could read. He thought he was fulfilling his calling by preaching two very good sermons on Sundays and by baptizing, marrying and burying the local Americans of Scotch descent on weekdays. The

*''Retrievers Good and Bad'' by Norman Maclean is reprinted from *Esquire* 88 (October 1977), pp. 22, 30, 32, 34, 36. Copyright © 1977 by Norman Maclean.

so-called church work he regarded as woman's work, and so it was my mother who visited the new members of the church and ran the Ladies' Aid and Christian Endeavor and tried to sing louder than anyone else in the congregation.

My father's ideas about a duck dog were highly specialized. He expected the dog to be totally his from the opening morning of duck season until the closing sunset. During the remaining portion of the year, he expected the dog to be taken care of, as the church was, by God and my mother, but in the case of the dog, God with some justification left the work to my mother. So she fed the dog all year until hunting season, she combed and brushed it, and she saw that the dog had a good bed and clean bedding. She even watched— more closely than my father—the coming date of the opening of the duck season; a month before, she would confine the dog to the garage because she knew my father was not unique among mankind in expecting to have a duck dog on opening day even though he hadn't taken care of it until then. Any dog resembling a duck dog, any dog even with yellow eyes, could not venture alone on the streets of my town two weeks or even a month before the opening of the season without being—not exactly stolen—but abducted until November 30. So my mother locked up the dog and then of course she had to walk it.

My mother was a fine working woman, but she had one short-coming. She ran the church and all that, she had a family to take care of and she was stableboy, as it were, for a succession of large female Chesapeake Bay retrievers. But she was not a dog trainer, and my father on the opening day of duck season expected not only a well-fed and well-kept dog but a perfect retriever. Since he would not train the dogs himself, it may be difficult to understand just how he expected them to show instantaneous perfection, but this is what he expected of hunting dogs and firstborn sons.

My father's interest in the dog business was more theological than scientific, so if a dog did not approach perfection, we got another Chesapeake Bay retriever for the next season. They were always called Fanny, a name I did not like, and the dogs never particularly liked me, but my father always said they were mine. This process went on long after I left home and included dogs that I practically never saw, but it is easy to understand how in over thirty years I came to own a kennel, as it were, of "almost duck dogs" and even one dog that on her own power approached perfection. Then, finally, there was a dog that was not given to me.

I realize that my father and my town were fairly special, but it's a good guess that something like what went on in my town went on in most small towns that were near shooting water. Universal pulsations seem to spread among ducks and duck hunters alike. It is said that far north in Canada, in the marshes where the ducks nest, you can hear increasing restlessness both day and night some weeks before the migrations begin, even if there is no visible sign of the storms that finally set the ducks off. And, at the same time, south of the border, there is a stirring all along main streets when something like a duck dog—even a cocker spaniel—goes by. Doors flutter open, sales are postponed, and customers and salesmen alike, especially hardware salesmen who sell shotgun shells, come out on the walk and suddenly become dog fanciers. It is almost a sure bet, too, that not one of the dogs, even those with good bloodlines, is well trained. It takes time to train a dog—summertime—and in summertime the duck hunters and hardware salesmen I knew went fishing, including, of course, my father, who even tied his own flies. Come autumn, a dog hasn't much choice but to rely on his blood, which, given my experience, is never quite enough.

The almost duck dog whose genetic deficiencies aroused my father most was Fanny II. By the time I acquired title to her, we had moved to western Montana, where there was excellent duck shooting and where for the first time my father was tempted to shoot over his legal limit. Accordingly, he started taking me with him, although I was scarcely as long as the castoff double-barrel shotgun I kept stumbling over and not half so powerful, at least in reverse. Naturally, my father didn't take me along to shoot ducks. I was too young to have to buy a license, and all the ducks over the twenty he shot (twenty was the limit then) I was given to carry. They were mine—along with the dog. The dog, when I try honestly to remember, looked like any other Chesapeake Bay retriever—big, with brown curly hair, yellow eyes, intelligent, professional. We were shooting in an outlet of a lake, quiet water covered with dead reeds, stuff that looked to me like seaweed and muck of that sort. Every time my father dropped a bird in the water, Fanny II would charge out and, swimming high, would shoulder the dead duck aside and, four or five feet beyond, snap a mouthful of floating seaweed. She had a passion for seaweed, and with an almost sexual smile on her face she would return it to my father. Then, still standing right in front of him and still untrained, she would shake all the water out of her coat, most of which he had to absorb.

After a while he asked me if I would take off my clothes and swim for the ducks, and I did, but I hated it. It was all kind of marshy stuff, and I had to pull my legs through ooze a foot or more deep, dragging bubbles behind me, and when I swam I could feel things touching my body. I was exhausted by the end of the day and hoped that my father would soon get rid of the dog. I needn't have worried about my father. He regarded the dog as an anti-duck dog and even as an antichristian. It wasn't the dog's retrieving seaweed that was sacrilege to my father; it was her pushing the dead duck aside. You can be sure that it was the only day we ever hunted with Fanny II.

I tend to remember best the almost duck dogs that enraged my father most. One made him swear—the only time I ever heard him do so. This Fanny was rather late in the succession, and by the time I acquired ownership, I was going with a girl whose home was in Wolf Creek, which is only a few miles from the Missouri River and not too far from its headwaters. Even there it is a big river and looks as big or even bigger than it does six or seven hundred miles farther down. It is still clear but is powerful and full of undercurrents and big bends against cliffs. It was just below the fabled canyon named the Gates of the Mountains by Lewis and Clark.

My father had hunted several seasons with this dog and evidently had found her satisfactory, but he had hunted with her in the quiet oozy outlet where seaweed drifts by that I described earlier. Well, there is no seaweed drifting on the Big Missouri, where we were shooting. The Missouri is one of the main flyways for ducks in America, and when the autumn storms begin in the north, the ducks come whistling out of Canada, hit the Missouri River, follow it to the Mississippi and coast the rest of the way to Louisiana. When they go around those big bends on the upper Missouri, the air is left hurt and shaking, and if you are a duck hunter, the place to be is behind a rock on the cliffside of the bends, because the ducks' speed on the turns almost drives them into the cliffs and into your gun barrel. That is just where my father and I were.

My father was in good form, and we knocked down several ducks so close to shore that we almost could have retrieved them without a dog. Then a stray came by making such faint vibrations that he passed us before we saw him. We both fired, and he hit the water at least halfway across the river, but the dog had seen him and started out. The trouble was she was used to retrieving in quiet water, and she should have run down the river bank a lot farther before starting to swim for the duck because the current carried the duck a long way before the dog caught up with it. In fact, the duck by then was nearer the other bank, so the dog gave an extra snap of her neck to set the duck securely in place and then just kept going—for the other side.

I have a theory—probably not subscribed to by academic geneticists—that just as Chesapeakes are coded for retrieving, Scotchmen are coded for profanity. Not obscenity, just profanity. I have known quite a few Scotchmen in my time, including my father's brother, so this has to be taken at least as a considered opinion. I always felt that my father lived a somewhat unnatural and unhappy life because he could not swear, but once, to my knowledge, he showed his genetic tape.

He leaned his shotgun against the rock and stood up, scaring off a big flight that had started to make the bend, but he never noticed it. "Goodness!" he said, which is as far as he usually descended into the abyss. Then he said, "My goodness." Then he exploded: "Do you see that damn dog over there?" It was a hell of a long way off, but I could see the bitch lying on a sandbar with what looked like a big fat mallard between her paws. I believe that if my father thought his gun could have carried the river, he would have given the dog both barrels. After a good rest she came swimming back, without the duck, and if you are interested in things that give the appearance of being a long way off, take a good look at a duck you have shot that's lying dead forever on the other side of the Missouri.

Fortunately, the dog handled most of the rest of the ducks fairly well, but she carried four or five more across the river and left them there—which was enough to spoil the day for my father. I am glad to say, though, that the experience left no lasting marks on any of us. That evening my Wolf Creek girl and I had several good laughs, and a little later in life we were married and lived happily for many years. My father forgave the dog and hunted with her for a number of seasons—but always on quiet water. It might have been simpler if he had trained her to recognize that he was the center of the universe and that all things falling into the water were to be returned to him, he being, as it were, the Creator. It wouldn't have been hard.

Our almost-perfect duck dog was our last Chesapeake—as if genetics had arranged itself in dramatic and climactic order. She was bigger than our other dogs and more imperial. When my father started me fly-fishing, there were only about a dozen flies that any trout fisherman carried with him—plain and royal coachmen, grey hackles with red or yellow bodies, brown hackles and my favorite— if only for its name—Queen of Waters. To me, this dog was Queen of Waters. I wish that she could have found it in her heart to return a little of the feeling I had for her, but she did not care for me particularly or for my father or even for my mother or ducks or even dead ducks. She was my first encounter with a strict professional. She loved only one thing—she loved to do the thing she could do, which was to bring in dead ducks.

She made that Missouri River look like an irrigation ditch. Sometimes, while the rest of the world lies turning in bed and counting sheep, I lie turning in bed and counting the ducks she brought in for us the first day we worked her on the Missouri. It was as cold as hell and the ducks were being projected from Canada as if from a rocket base, but she missed nothing that skidded upon the waters. We were hunting with two other parties, each of which had a spaniel, and by nine o'clock in the morning both spaniels were through. The big water and the undercurrents and the cold had finished them off. There could be five dead ducks floating down the river and the dogs would only put a foot in the water and whine. Finally, their owners took them back to the car and wrapped them in blankets. Even in the bitter cold of the late-afternoon shooting, the Queen of Waters was still retrieving the ducks for my father and me and the other two parties. It was so cold by then that long icicles hung from her brown curls. I can still hear her rushing by me for the river, tinkling like a glass chandelier in a windstorm, and I can go to sleep with this sound in my ears.

This dog was great even when she goofed. Actually, I can remember her goofing only once, and then she almost killed my father, me and herself. Not just one or two of us—the works. She swung only in the larger orbits. This was the first season she had been shot over, and we were shooting on a slough on the Blackfoot River. There were a good many ducks on the water when we sneaked into our blind around daybreak, and we got three of them when they rose off the water. The dog hit the slough as if she had come out of a cannon, but even so, she hadn't got the three ducks to shore before another flight circled, started to light, then saw the dog and took off before my father had a shot. This is a good slough, and for an hour or so after daybreak there is a big movement of ducks over it, so it is best not to send your dog out on the water until the flights start easing off. Well, the Queen of Waters, although still but a large pup, was doing her thing and in the process she scared another flight that had started to settle. Finally my father fumbled in the pockets of his hunting jacket, pulled out a long piece of stout cord, softly called her and tied her to him, from her collar to his leg. Then he looked shyly at me to see if I had been watching.

This slough is in deep woods, and usually you hear the ducks coming in before you see them. I didn't even hear the ducks this time, but I saw the dog stiffen and I kept raising my eyes. I saw my father swing his gun to his shoulder and then I saw a duck swerve out of the flock, and in a moment you could project the duck's curve to the water. The moment you could, the dog could, too, and the cord held. She started for the water like a supercharged dray horse, hauling my father's leg through the reeds. My father didn't freeze on the trigger because the gun was a semiautomatic and if he had frozen on the trigger he would have fired only once. Instead, he must have gone into a state of convulsions, and his gun was blazing. One shot went through the reeds and laid down a swath as if he were mowing hay. Then he just missed me and then he just missed the dog and once, I am sure, he almost shot himself. It scared the hell out of me, but I lived to verify the accuracy of the old western description of a charge of shot going past your head as ''busting a hole in the breeze.'' Shakily, I got my father unwound from the reeds and the dog and the cord and his gun, but even before I had totally completed this operation and certainly before I had quit shaking, I heard the spraying of water on reeds, and there was the dog with the duck.

She was a magnificent creation and had a privilege not granted to many mortals—of living long enough to approach perfection. Then, shortly after these things happened to the dog, my brother was murdered. I try to say it the way it was—without premonition, never to be explained and never to be assimilated. It had no past and it never went on and turned into something else. It just was— suddenly, shockingly and forever.

After the funeral my father and mother and I spent several weeks at our cabin on the lake. It was early May, and the forest floor of the cathedral of thousand-year-old tamaracks was covered with dog-tooth violets, which are really lilies. Around the lake they are often called glacier lilies, probably because it is only about twenty miles from our lake to the glaciers. We thought they were the most beautiful and fragile flowers we would ever see, and we tried not to walk on any of them.

My father aged rapidly. He never hunted ducks again and had to give up most of his trout fishing. His feet dragged when he walked, as if his leg muscles had atrophied, so he could not fish the big rivers any more or even the creeks that were hard to get to. Mostly, he fished in the lake in front of our cabin in a flat-bottomed boat he had made many years before. If it was bright, he wore no hat, and his almost-red Scotch hair paled until it became part of the sunlight. If it was at all cool, he wore one of my brother's fishing jackets, and soon after my brother's death he adopted his dog. My brother's dog was a handsome springer spaniel called Quake because my brother had got him as a pup in 1935, the year of the earthquake in Helena. My brother had been a fine shot with a scatter-gun, and Quake was a very good duck dog—not as professional a duck dog as the Queen of Waters, but in the end the best dog of all.

This dog and my father greatly changed each other's lives. The dog and my father were inseparable, whereas before, my father cared to be with dogs only during the hunting season. As for the dog, I am sure there are other cases like his, but he was the only dog I ever saw that became another dog for love of another man. For my brother he had been a duck dog, and now for my father he became a fishing dog, if one can speak of such a species. He would sit all day in the boat on the seat next to my father and peer into the impenetrable water. He not only loved but admired my father greatly—I am sure he thought the whole fishing thing was completely under my father's control, as I did when I was the dog's age and believed my father could come up with a fish whenever he was so minded. After staring a respectable length of time into the water without seeing anything but pieces of sunlight, he would bark at my father, and when my father caught a fish, the dog would lick my father's whole face, though my father still needed part of it to see how to unhook the fish.

To the others in my family, the dog was something of a sacred object that had prolonged my father's life and helped to steady the rest of us. He was a fine dog, and after him, my father had no other dog.

The Hidden Art
of a Good Story:
Wallace Stegner Lecture

Norman Maclean*

    I am deeply touched to find myself here in Lewiston, Idaho where the Clearwater River runs into the Snake. I feel as if much of my life for a long time has been flowing this way, and finally it got here. Nearly 70 years ago, when I was about the same age as many of you who are students, I started spending summers working for the United States Forest Service on the Selway and Lochsa Rivers, headwaters of the Clearwater. There were no roads back there then and in many places only game trails that soon petered out, often in high mountain meadows where the huckleberry bushes were covered with the white belly-hair of mountain goats that had been feeding there. I spent three summers crossing the Bitterroot Mountains into this part of Idaho from the Montana side, and I transferred from there to the Kootenai Forest only because I then thought I would enter the Forest Service as my life profession and so should be moving around and seeing many different forests of the north-west.

But the three summers I spent in the headwaters of the Clear-water were one of the most formative times of my life. Things were happening fast to me then that help to explain why I came to write and what I wrote about and how I wrote and why I am here. The last story in the volume of my stories entitled *A River Runs Through It* is the long story with the title, "USFS 1919: The Ranger, The Cook, and a Hole in the Sky." The opening paragraphs of this story will give you a clear sense of how formative that time was for me:

> And then he thinks he knows
> The hills where his life rose . . .
> —Matthew Arnold,
> "The Buried Life"

I was young and I thought I was tough and I knew it was beautiful and I was a little bit crazy but hadn't noticed it yet. Outside the ranger station there were more moun-tains in all directions than I was ever to see again—oceans of mountains—and inside the station at this particular mo-ment I was ahead in a game of cribbage with the ranger of the Elk Summit District of the Selway Forest of the United States Forest Service (USFS), which was even younger than I was and enjoyed many of the same char-acteristics.

It was mid-August of 1919, so I was seventeen and the Forest Service was only fourteen, since, of several possible birthdays for the Forest Service, I pick 1905, when the Forest Division of the Department of the Interior was transferred to the Department of Agriculture and named the United States Forest Service.

In 1919 it was twenty-eight miles from the Elk Summit Ranger Station of the Selway Forest to the nearest road, fourteen miles to the top of the Bitterroot Divide and fourteen straight down Blodgett Canyon to the Bitterroot Valley only a few miles from Hamilton, Montana. The fourteen miles going down were as cruel as the fourteen going up, and far more dangerous, since Blodgett Canyon was medically famous for the tick that gave Rocky Mountain Fever, with one chance out of five for recovery. The twenty-eight mile trail from Elk Summit to the mouth of Blodgett Canyon was a Forest Service trail and therefore marked by a blaze with a notch on top; only a few other trails in the vast Elk Summit district were so marked. Otherwise, there were only game trails and old trappers' trails that gave out on open ridges and meadows with no signs of where the game or trappers had vanished. It was a world of strings of pack horses or men who walked alone—a world of hoof and foot and the rest done by hand. Nineteen nineteen across the Bitterroot Divide in northern Idaho was just before the end of most of history that had had no four-wheel drives, no bulldozers, no power saws and nothing pneumatic to take the place of jackhammers and nothing chemical or airborne to put out forest fires.

Nowadays you can scarcely be a lookout without a uniform and a college degree, but in 1919 not a man in our outfit, least of all the ranger himself, had been to college. They still picked rangers for the Forest Service by picking the toughest guy in town. Ours, Bill Bell, was the toughest in the Bitterroot Valley, and we thought he was the best ranger in the Forest Service. We were strengthened in this belief by the rumor that Bill had killed a sheepherder. We were a little disappointed that he had been acquitted of the charges, but nobody held it against him, for we all knew that being acquitted of killing a sheepherder in Montana isn't the same as being innocent.

One seeming side-effect of my early family training was that I learned a great deal about literature by hearing it read, with the result that I depend heavily upon sound to guide me in my writing.

I write by paragraphs which I hear as units of sound that rise a few notes to their middle, then drop a note or two as the paragraph comes to an end—except right at the very end when they rise a note or two to start the next paragraph, slightly higher in the scale than the preceding paragraph, and so help quietly to increase the scale of interest as the story proceeds. I need hardly tell you that families no longer read to each other. I am sure it leaves a sound-gap in family life.

I might add that I learned a great deal about the sound of literature in the Forest Service by listening to story-tellers around the camp-fire at night and I will speak before I finish more precisely about some of what I learned about literature by camp-fires.

Although all this was long ago and I was young, those three summers I spent in the headwaters of the Clearwater gave a shape to what was to become my character and pointers to the directions my writing would follow the rest of my life. I should like to trace some of these just as they were taking shape, when in some ways they are easier to see than when they become more mature and take on complexities that make them probably more interesting but also probably more difficult to discern analytically. I propose, then, to show you some of the basic qualities of my present writing that were hardening into shape when I was between 17 and 19 years old and was working with mountain men and trying to be one myself in the great mountains that lie between the headwaters of our common river here and the Bitterroot Mountains. Besides me, there was nothing there but mountains and mountain men, and I promised myself that some day I would write about them, and I have. I should like to illustrate what I have to say by reading from stories I did not write until after I retired at 73.

What is most basic to my writing comes in a cluster. The most basic of this cluster comes from the fact that for the first time in my life I was working with men and men who were masters in the arts of the woods. Up to then, I had lived the life of a lonely boy, in a room across from my father's study in the mornings and in the afternoons usually by myself in the woods. But at 17, I walked behind a pack train pulling out of Blodgett Canyon bound for the mountains of Idaho. There was a gigantic fire ahead and no other way to get a crew and its supplies there except by mule and horse and foot. It was a huge operation. In the morning the horses and mules were saddled—30 or 40 of them. Bill Bell, the head packer (who was also ranger), stood on one side of the trail, his assistant packer on the other side, and the string of pack animals was slowly led between them. They slowed but never stopped walking while the head packer hoisted one pack and cinched it to the saddle and on the other side the assistant packer did the same with his. The packs were so balanced in weight that the animals never had sores on their backs because their load was never lopsided, and it never slipped, no matter how tough the going ahead. And ahead were great cliffs spotted all over with white spots of mountain goats and at the end of the canyon were the great switchbacks rising to cross the Bitterroot divide to Idaho. There were triangles getting smaller and smaller until far ahead there was only one horse and one rider disappearing into the sky—the head packer. And at the turns of the switchbacks the saddles and cinches groaned and the horses and mules left great piles of manure and shook in their packs to keep things steady. I was young and I suppose over-prone to hero worship, but when I saw the packstring ascend in triangles until the head packer disappeared into the sky, I formed a lifelong ambition— I wanted to be a head packer, and still do. Except that with four-wheel drives and helicopters, there isn't much left to do for packers except to take rich dudes and carpetbaggers from the east on camping trips to the Bob Marshall Wilderness.

But that is the way it was for me—a young romantic beginning an involvement and commitment to life and writing which—when it reached its most enlarged and present state—rests on the basic belief that what seems most beautiful in all I see about me is what men and women can create with their hands, issuing from their hearts and heads. I can't go by a building site where they are excavating without stopping to watch the great crane coming down and picking up a great clawful of dirt and coming to the top of the construction with such precision and grace that you would think a seamstress was guiding it on the way. It roars going up but only whispers as it is laid to rest. Stated more formally, as if for class-room consumption, basically I am a recorder, an historian of the arts that skilled men and women can perform with their hands, especially on the area of this earth's surface where I was brought up and where I should know what I am talking about.

I have already said three basic characteristics come in clusters, so it would be difficult to illustrate one without also being aware of the several others that can accompany it and contribute to whatever power it may have. A second one I must put the finger on imme-diately is that, for me, it is not enough to make just a precise ob-jective description of how to cast a fly-rod or how to land a big fish or for that matter how to lose a big fish or how to pack a mule so mountain trails won't make it slip. Dan Bailey, the great fly fish-erman and fly tyer, whose great national store was in Livingston, Montana, often said, judging from the number of reports of what he said came to me, "There are hundreds of books and articles on how to fly fish, but only Maclean tells you how it feels." As a teacher, I have written a great deal in which I have just put things on the dotted line and said, "there they are." I even have been co-author of a book on *Military Maps and Aerial Photographs*, but I come to you as a story-teller, therefore something of an artist, and if you ask me, something of a poet. In the many years that I taught I taught far more courses in poetry—in lyric poetry—than in the nar-rative forms of the novel or short story, and of course far more than I taught in bibliography. Only the poetry I see, I deeply believe, is in reality. I am gifted enough so I can see it there but, I am happy to say, not gifted enough to make it up with pretty images and extended metaphors. After all, I do not speak, at least in private, of "A River Runs Through It" as a story about the tragedy of my family—among my friends, I speak of it "as my love poem to my family."

One more basic characteristic has to be added to the close cluster of basic characteristics of my love poem to my family or to my love of the earth's surface between Montana and Idaho. Long before I became a student of the beauty and art of what men and women can do with their hands, I was deeply aware of the beauty and designs of nature. I suppose that would be natural enough, turned loose in nature nearly every afternoon. I suppose it was only natural that nature became my one close friend I had outside of my family. I came to regard it as something like a member of my family. I loved it, and I thought it made sense. I thought, like the works of men and women, it had design and structure and beauty to it. I also thought if I only stayed still and looked hard and thought about what I had seen I could see how it was connected with the beauty of what men and women could do with their hands and heart and head. I never had a course in geology, but early I became a fairly good home-grown geologist. I could tell you why long stretches of the Blackfoot River were on the south side of the valley and why 1000 feet above there were large rock outcroppings that had long horizontal gashes on them and why, generally speaking, there were three parts to a good fishing hole and how they came to be and how eventually these parts all came together in a river, that, like the art of men and women, has shape, and design, and rhythm, and sweeps from one side of the valley to the other in an artistic curve. As it says at the end of the story, "A River Runs Through It": "All things merge into one and a river runs through it."

The stories, then, in this collection of short stories, *A River Runs Though It*, rest on three closely related aspirations: (1) to depict the art and grace of what men and women can do with their hands in the region of the country that I was brought up in and know best; (2) to impart with a description of these arts something of the feeling that accompanies their performance or, indeed, of intelligently watching them performed; and (3) of seeing in the parts of nature where they were performed something like the beauty, structure, rhythm and design of the arts themselves. I can illustrate these related aspirations with two passages from "USFS 1919":

> To take a pack string of nearly half a hundred across the Bitterroot Divide was to perform a masterpiece in that now almost lost art, and in 1919 I rode with Bill Bell and saw it done.
>
> The divide was just as beautiful as the way up. In Au-

gust it was blue with June lupine. Froth dropped off the jaws of the horses and mules, and, snorting through enlarged red nostrils, the animals shook their saddles, trying without hands to rearrange their loads. Not far to the south was El Capitan, always in snow and always living up to its name. Ahead and to the west was our ranger station—and the mountains of Idaho, poems of geology stretching beyond any boundaries and seemingly even beyond the world.

Six miles or so west of the divide is a lake, roughly two-thirds of the way between Hamilton and Elk Summit, that is the only place where there is water and enough grass to hold a big bunch of horses overnight. K. D. Swan, the fine photographer of the early Forest Service, should have been there to record the design of the divide—ascending in triangles to the sky and descending in ovals and circles to an oval meadow and an oval lake with a moose knee-deep beside lily pads. It was triangles going up and ovals coming down, and on the divide it was springtime in August.

The unpacking was just as beautiful—one wet satin back after another without saddle or saddle sore, and not a spot of white wet flesh where hair and hide had rubbed off. Perhaps one has to know something about keeping packs balanced on the backs of animals to think this beautiful, or to notice it at all, but to all those who work come moments of beauty unseen by the rest of the world.

So, to a horseman who has to start looking for horses before daybreak, nothing is so beautiful in darkness as the sound of a bell mare.

*   *   *

In the late afternoon, of course, the mountains meant all business for the lookouts. The big winds were veering from the valleys toward the peaks, and smoke from little fires that had been secretly burning for several days might show up for the first time. New fires sprang out of thunder before it sounded. By three-thirty or four, the lightning would be flexing itself on the distant ridges like a fancy prizefighter, skipping sideways, ducking, showing off but not hitting anything. By four-thirty or five, it was another game. You could feel the difference in the air that had become hard to breathe. The lightning now came walking into you, delivering short smashing punches. With an alidade, you marked a line on the map toward where it struck and started counting, "Thousand-one, thousand-two," and so on, putting in the "thousand" to slow your count to a second each time. If the thunder reached you at "thousand-five," you figured the lightning had struck about a mile away. The punches became shorter and the count closer and you knew you were going to take punishment. Then the lightning and thunder struck together. There was no count.

But what I remember best is crawling out of the tent on summer nights when on high mountains autumn is always approaching. To a boy, it is something new and beautiful to piss among the stars. Not under the stars but among them. Even at night great winds seem always to blow on great mountains, and tops of trees bend, but, as the boy stands there with nothing to do but to watch, seemingly the sky itself bends and the stars blow down through the trees until the Milky Way becomes lost in some distant forest. As the cosmos brushes by the boy and disappears among the trees, the sky is continually replenished with stars. There would be stars enough to brush by him all night, but by now the boy is getting cold.

Then the shivering organic speck of stream itself disappears.

I have made a change in direction from what I planned to say next to you tonight. I had planned to go on to other characteristics of my stories that might be of some help to you—at least of some interest—but in mid-flight I decided that this cluster of three big basics was enough and more might only clog the machinery. I also decided that just reading you a couple of short excerpts from my stories would give only a jerky introduction to them with no sense of their flow and movement and rhythm—and a story, if anything, is flow and movement and rhythm. Much of the story-art is in the hidden art of keeping the story flowing.

So what I am going to do is read a section of my best-known story, "A River Runs Through It." It is the scene where we see my brother for the last time in the story, and from this scene it moves to the last scene in the story, the scene of his death. This section next to last begins with the scene of his landing the last big fish. One principle of progression in the story is the order in which you learn about the art of fly-fishing, from the initial scene in which my brother and I as boys are taught the art of casting a fly rod. The next time you see my brother he is doing what you would do next—picking out the water he is going to fish, quite an important part of the art. Only one aspect of the art of fly-fishing is presented each time you see him fish—the human mind does well to absorb one technical aspect of art at a time. After the fly-casting scene, you next see him choosing what fly he is to fish with. This of course includes a scene where he is closely reading the water and the bushes on the shore to figure out what flies are hatching—whether they are amphibian insects hatching out of shallow water or terrestrials hatching out of the alder bushes. And so on—one fishing trip for one lesson in the art of fly-fishing until we come, finally, to the last one—landing a fish. That will be where I start reading. It seemed to me that the last time you saw my brother, the master fisherman, he should be landing his last big fish.

Fans who know a good deal about fly fishing and rivers also know something about literature and have written me to say that without making any fuss about it, the book—among other things—is a complete manual in the art of fly fishing from soup to nuts so to speak—from how to cast and get your fly on the water to how to get your fish out of the water. I believe very much in what I call hidden art—art in which the reader doesn't quite see what you have done—he only feels it's a good story.

Since I'm at the mouth of the Clearwater, I don't mind revealing to close friends a few trade secrets. Although I realized that viewing my brother close at hand as he fought his last big fish would have certain advantages, I decided dead against it. I decided he should be seen so far away he could not be seen as an individual. I decided he should start fading away as an individual existence just before he faded away forever. I also wanted toward the end for him to fade away as a body and become as befitted a master fisherman: just an abstract in the art of fishing in the most climactic act of the art—landing a big fish. I will read now the next to last scene of the story, and I will say not a word about the last scene, his death. If there is any art to it, let it remain hidden and be buried with him.

The voices of the subterranean river in the shadows were different from the voices of the sunlit river ahead. In the shadows against the cliff the river was deep and engaged in profundities, circling back on itself now and then to say things over to be sure it had understood itself. But the river ahead came out into the sunny world like a chatterbox, doing its best to be friendly. It bowed to one shore and then to the other so nothing would feel neglected.

By now I could see inside the sunshine and had located my father. He was sitting high on the bank. He wore no hat. Inside the sunlight, his faded red hair was once again ablaze and again in glory. He was reading, although evidently only by sentences because he often looked away from the book. He did not close the book until some time after he saw me.

I scrambled up the bank and asked him, "How many did you get?" He said, "I got all I want." I said, "But how many did you get?" He said, "I got four or five." I asked, "Are they any good?" He said, "They are beautiful."

He was about the only man I ever knew who used the

world "beautiful" as a natural form of speech, and I guess I picked up the habit from hanging around him when I was little.

"How many did you catch?" he asked. "I also caught all I want," I told him. He omitted asking me just how many that was, but he did ask me, "Are they any good?" "They are beautiful," I told him, and sat down beside him.

"What have you been reading?" I asked. "A book," he said. It was on the ground on the other side of him. So I would not have to bother to look over his knees to see it, he said, "A good book."

Then he told me, "In the part I was reading it says the Word was in the beginning, and that's right. I used to think water was first, but if you listen carefully you will hear that the words are underneath the water."

"That's because you are a preacher first and then a fisherman," I told him. "If you ask Paul, he will tell you that the words are formed out of water."

"No," my father said, "you are not listening carefully. The water runs over the words. Paul will tell you the same thing. Where is Paul anyway?"

I told him he had gone back to fish the first hole over again. "But he promised to be here soon," I assured him. "He'll be here when he catches his limit," he said. "He'll be here soon," I reassured him, partly because I could already see him in the subterranean shadows.

My father went back to reading and I tried to check what we had said by listening. Paul was fishing fast, picking up one here and there and wasting no time in walking them to shore. When he got directly across from us, he held up a finger on each hand and my father said, "He needs two more for his limit."

I looked to see where the book was left open and knew just enough Greek to recognize λόγος as the Word. I guessed from it and the argument that I was looking at the first verse of John. While I was looking, Father said, "He has one on."

It was hard to believe, because he was fishing in front of us on the other side of the hole that Father had just fished. Father slowly rose, found a good-sized rock and held it behind his back. Paul landed the fish, and waded out again for number twenty and his limit. Just as he was making the first cast, Father threw the rock. He was old enough so that he threw awkwardly and afterward had to rub his shoulder, but the rock landed in the river about where Paul's fly landed and at about the same time, you can see where my brother learned to throw rocks into his partner's fishing water when he couldn't bear to see his partner catch any more fish.

Paul was startled for only a moment. Then he spotted Father on the bank rubbing his shoulder, and Paul laughed, shook his fist at him, backed to shore and went downstream until he was out of rock range. From there he waded into the water and began to cast again, but now he was far enough away so we couldn't see his line or loops. He was a man with a wand in a river, and whatever happened we had to guess from what the man and the wand and the river did.

As he waded out, his big right arm swung back and forth. Each circle of his arm inflated his chest. Each circle was faster and higher and longer until his arm became defiant and his chest breasted the sky. On shore we were sure, although we could see no line, that the air above him was singing with loops of line that never touched the water but got bigger and bigger each time they passed and sang. And we knew what was in his mind from the lengthening defiance of his arm. He was not going to let his fly touch any water close to shore where the small and middle-sized fish were. We knew from his arm and chest that all parts of him were saying, "No small one for the last one." Everything was going into one big cast for one last big fish.

From our angle high on the bank, my father and I could see where in the distance the wand was going to let the fly first touch water. In the middle of the river was a rock iceberg, just its tip exposed above water and underneath it a rock house. It met all the residential requirements for big fish—powerful water carrying food to the front and back doors, and rest and shade behind them.

My father said, "There has to be a big one out there."

I said, "A little one couldn't live out there."

My father said, "The big one wouldn't let it."

My father could tell by the width of Paul's chest that he was going to let the next loop sail. It couldn't get any wider. "I wanted to fish out there," he said, "but I couldn't cast that far."

Paul's body pivoted as if he were going to drive a golf ball three hundred yards, and his arm went high into the great arc and the tip of his wand bent like a spring, and then everything sprang and sang.

Suddenly, there was an end of action. The man was immobile. There was no bend, no power in the wand. It pointed at ten o'clock and ten o'clock pointed at the rock. For a moment the man looked like a teacher with a pointer illustrating something about a rock to a rock. Only water moved. Somewhere above the top of the rock house a fly was swept in water so powerful only a big fish could be there to see it.

Then the universe stepped on its third rail. The wand jumped convulsively as it made contact with the magic current of the world. The wand tried to jump out of the man's right hand. His left hand seemed to be frantically waving goodbye to a fish, but actually was trying to throw enough line into the rod to reduce the voltage and ease the shock of what had struck.

Everything seemed electrically charged but electrically unconnected. Electrical sparks appeared here and there on the river. A fish jumped so far downstream that it seemed

outside the man's electrical field, but, when the fish had
jumped, the man had leaned back on the rod and it was
then that the fish had toppled back into the water not
guided in its reentry by itself. The connections between
the convulsions and the sparks became clearer by repetition. When the man leaned back on the wand and the fish
reentered the water not altogether under its own power,
the wand recharged with convulsions, the man's hand
waved frantically at another departure, and much farther
below a fish jumped again. Because of the connections, it
became the same fish.

The fish made three such long runs before another act
in the performance began. Although the act involved a big
man and a big fish, it looked more like children playing.
The man's left hand sneakily began recapturing line, and
then, as if caught in the act, threw it all back into the rod
as the fish got wise and made still another run.

"He'll get him," I assured my father.

"Beyond doubt," my father said. The line going out
became shorter than what the left hand took in.

When Paul peered into the water behind him, we knew
he was going to start working the fish to shore and didn't
want to back into a hole or rock. We could tell he had
worked the fish into shallow water because he held the rod
higher and higher to keep the fish from bumping into anything on the bottom. Just when we thought the performance was over, the wand convulsed and the man thrashed
through the water after some unseen power departing for
the deep.

"The son of a bitch still has fight in him," I thought I
said to myself, but unmistakably I said it out loud, and
was embarrassed for having said it out loud in front of my
father. He said nothing.

Two or three more times Paul worked him close to shore,
only to have him swirl and return to the deep, but even at
that distance my father and I could feel the ebbing of the

underwater power. The rod went high in the air, and the man moved backwards swiftly but evenly, motions which when translated into events meant the fish had tried to rest for a moment on top of the water and the man had quickly raised the rod high and skidded him to shore before the fish thought of getting under the water again. He skidded him across the rocks clear back to a sandbar before the shocked fish gasped and discovered he could not live in oxygen. In belated despair, he rose in the sand and consumed the rest of momentary life dancing the Dance of Death on his tail.

The man put the wand down, got on his hands and knees in the sand, and, like an animal, circled another animal and waited. Then the shoulder shot straight out, and my brother stood up, faced us, and, with uplifted arm proclaimed himself the victor. Something giant dangled from his fist. Had Romans been watching they would have thought that what was dangling had a helmet on it.

"That's his limit," I said to my father.

"He is beautiful," my father said, although my brother had just finished catching his limit in the hole my father had already fished.

This was the last fish we were ever to see Paul catch. My father and I talked about this moment several times later, and whatever our other feelings, we always felt it fitting that, when we saw him catch his last fish, we never saw the fish but only the artistry of the fisherman.

'Billiards Is a Good Game': Gamesmanship and America's First Nobel Prize Scientist

Norman Maclean*

When I came here in 1928, now more than half the history of the University ago, the University of Chicago was the one institution of higher learning that was thought to exist west of the Appalachians by the populace east of the Appalachians. This widespread recognition was based largely on the names of Leopold and Loeb, Clarence Darrow (who in the eastern mind was also connected with the University of Chicago), A. A. Stagg, and Albert Abraham Michelson, who in 1907 had been the first American to win the Nobel Prize in science. Before arriving on campus, I may also have heard of Arthur Holly Compton, because only the year before he had been awarded the Nobel Prize, but I have the feeling I did not know of him until I saw Mrs. Compton showing him off at intermissions in Mandel Hall.

Michelson and Einstein, however, were the best known scientists of the time—in some ways for almost opposite reasons, although both were physicists. Einstein was the wonder of the world because

*" 'Billiards Is a Good Game': Gamesmanship and America's First Nobel Prize Scientist" by Norman Maclean is reprinted from *The University of Chicago Magazine* 67 (Summer 1975), pp. 19–23. Copyright © 1975 by *The University of Chicago Magazine*. Reprinted by permission of the publisher.

he had encased the whole universe in a simple formula, $E = mc^2$, which we were told, equally wonderful to us, would be very upsetting if we could understand it. Especially to us who could not understand, he was the theorist beyond theorists.

Michelson's wonder was what his head did with his hands, and a few boxes and rotating mirrors. He measured things, especially things that were regarded as unmeasurable, ineffable, and precious as life itself. Among other things, he had measured light and a star. I watched him play billiards nearly every noon for several months before he retired from the University, and, in introducing myself, I could further say with equal truth, "Shake the hand that shook the hand of John L. Sullivan." If I get the right opening, though, I prefer saying, "When young, I watched Michelson play billiards."

Michelson's hands were to make many things that brought light to our universe, but nothing so marked him in the popular mind as his measurement of the speed of light itself. Throughout most of history, light had been thought of as instantaneous and present wherever there was nothing to cast a shadow, and probably throughout all history light will be thought of by poets and the rest of us as the source of body and soul, without which there would be no photosynthesis or food or love or moonlight in which to make love. Without light for a metaphor there would have been little poetry written and no candlelight to write it by. Christ said, "I am the light of the world," and Cardinal Newman's hymn to Him begins, "Lead, kindly light."

Michelson was to measure the speed of light many times (his most accurate figure being $186,285 \pm 2\frac{1}{2}$ miles per second) and modern electronic equipment has changed that figure to only 186,282.3960. When in 1878 as an ensign in Annapolis he made his first measurement he spent $10.00 of his own money to assemble his equipment (for $10.00 light measured 186,508 miles per second).

In 1928, three years before his death, everyone said of Michelson, "He measured light," and today he is one of the few Nobel Prize winners whom nearly all educated people can name and give the reason for the award, although Michelson's award actually was based on a wide spectrum of experiments. His youngest daughter showed her father's own sense of truth and artistry when she entitled her recent biography of him, *The Master of Light*. Of course, the fact that he was the first American to win the Nobel Prize in science helped to enshrine him both nationally and locally. Nowadays Nobel Prize winners at times seem to come a dime a dozen and every now and then in job-lots, two or three to an award, but for a long time in history there was none and then there was one and he was at the University of Chicago. President Harper himself had started the University on its long string of firsts—the first university to have a summer school, the first extension division organized as part of a university, the first university press to have its own press, and, certainly not least or last, the first university to have women on its faculty and a dean of women. But probably the University's two most unforgettable firsts go to Michelson for the first American Nobel Prize in science (1907) and to Enrico Fermi and his group for the first self-sustained nuclear reaction (1942). To include one of my old students, I'll add Jay Berwanger for the first Heisman Trophy (1935).

In 1928, when I first saw Michelson he was eating lunch at the Quadrangle Club, and I thought instantly of the opening of Carl Sandburg's poem, "I saw a famous man eating soup." One look at Michelson in old age and there could be no doubt that he was famous. He did not eat at the table reserved for the physicists. He ate at a table always reserved for him alone, and he occasionally smiled as he drew on his napkin. The waitress told us he drew sketches of the faculty he did not care to eat with. She said they all had long noses.

Few of us in these present days of unfamous and infamous men have any idea of what it was like to be one of the two or three most famous physicists of the early twentieth century and to eat your soup at a table reserved for you alone. The meaning of the words "elite" and "aristocratic" have been lost, except in their profane senses, and it is doubtful if we would recognize an aristocrat if there were one and we happened to see him. But at the first general open meeting in 1900 of the American Physical Society (of which Michelson was vice-president seven years before his Nobel Prize), its president, Henry Rowland, addressed his fellow members as follows:

> . . . We meet here in the interest of *a science above all sciences* which deals with the foundation of the Universe . . . with the constitution of matter from which everything in the Universe is made and with the ether of space by which alone the various portions of matter forming the Universe affect each other. . . .

> . . . We form a small and unique body of men, a new variety of the human race as one of our greatest scientists calls it, whose views of what constitutes the greatest achievement in life are very different from those around us. In this respect we form an aristocracy, not of wealth, not of pedigree, but of intellect and of ideals.

In case present-day readers might feel this prose is running over with self-anointed oil, they should start jotting down the names of some of the late-nineteenth and early-twentieth century physicists whom they and the world remember: Madame Curie and her husband, Pierre (radium and radioactivity), Lord Kelvin (as in Kelvinator), James Clerk Maxwell (electromagnetic field), Wilhelm Conrad Röntgen (X-rays), and, to end where we began, Einstein and Michelson. Every once in a while science comes to a place where it meets a bunch of great men coming its way who are big enough to overturn it and then set it on its wheels again but going forever in a different direction.

But his being the first American physicist to win the Nobel Prize still doesn't give us an adequate measurement of how high Michelson stood in the firmament of men apart from other men. Michelson was a Navy man. He had received his basic scientific training at Annapolis and it was better all around and forever after not to forget he had been a naval officer.

Shortly before anyone else in the dining room had finished his lunch, Michelson rose and went downstairs. Before long, I heard that he went down to the billiard room and probably at the same time I heard he was a fine billiard player. Nobody in the University, I was told, was good enough to play with him. Immediately, I started arriving earlier for lunch, and, when he folded his long-nosed napkin, I rose and followed him.

So for at least several months before he left Chicago for good, I sat on one of those high pool-room chairs for ten or fifteen minutes at noon and watched the famous physicist play billiards after he ate soup and sketched the ordinary self-anointed physicists with whom he did not sit. He and I occasionally spoke. Most of our communication, however, was carried on by a lifted eyebrow followed by a nod or shake of the head. He lifted the eyebrow, and I shook or nodded the head.

I had come here in 1928 to start graduate work with an A.B. in English from Dartmouth, and, since I had taught courses there in freshman English for two years after graduation, I was able to start here as a Graduate Assistant, a form of degradation that has since been abolished, at least in the English Department. As the first half of the title suggests, it was bestowed upon certain graduate students, but the second half of the title, "Assistant," gives no idea of how little money and how much servility went with it.

Only a few years later (in 1932), *Vanity Fair*, the magazine of the sophisticates (*The New Yorker* just getting under way), started publishing a series of caricatures by Covarrubias entitled "Impossible Interviews," the one that comes to mind first being between Mae West and Dowager-Queen Marie of Romania. If Covarrubias had seen the young Graduate Assistant in English and the great and aging physicist who was the first American Nobel Prize winner in science gathered each noon around a billiard table he might have included us in his series.

In 1928 there were two ways graduate students in English without money could see their way to an advanced degree, both involving considerable medical risk. Besides "the Graduate Assistant route," which was the scenic detour, there was the more common family way which was to marry a fellow graduate student, the marriage vows often consisting only of promises that each would take his or her turn in working on some job until the other received his or her Ph.D. In 1928 (as in 1975) it always fell out that it was the woman's turn first to give up her graduate studies and become the bread-winner. By the time the male finally fenced in a Ph.D., the female of the species had had so many children and jobs and was so generally worn-out (or dead) that it was too late for her and she could never bear to open a book again, except for pleasure.

The "Assistant" half of a Graduate Assistant needs a little more defining before one can appreciate the spectator as well as the billiard player in the coming scene. A Graduate Assistant, in addition to taking graduate courses, could teach up to three sections a quarter of the required course in English Composition at the rate of $200 per section. Financially, this meant that a Graduate Assistant who taught the full schedule of three sections for three quarters of a school year made $1,800. Since many of our freshman in 1928 were still from the rural Middle West, being a Graduate Assistant teaching three sections of English Composition spiritually meant going home late Friday afternoon, having a couple of shots of Prohibition gin, going to bed right after dinner and reading thirty (students) times three (sections) of one-thousand-word compositions on "How to Fill a Silo." By then, he was too weak to get out of bed, and besides he had to start preparing the graduate courses he was taking.

So the great difference between the two kinds of needy graduate students in English was in how they spent their weekends in bed. As a result of my weekends, I became an expert on corn, but my conversations with the great physicist were still limited to billiards.

For instance, we never mentioned bridge; yet I was soon to discover he hurried down to the billiard room before anyone else left upstairs because he wanted to play bridge but was not a good bridge player. Although he was too good at billiards to play with anybody in the club, none of the bridge players in the room next to the billiard tables wanted him for a partner. He coordinated these two facts by eating early, getting downstairs before anyone else, playing billiards by himself for ten or fifteen minutes, and then, just before the first big scraping of chairs upstairs, seating himself at the bridge table where there was room for just three others. But, though I also watched him play bridge, we never spoke about anything except billiards.

Undoubtedly, then, I would never have exchanged a single word with the Master of Light if I had not been brought up in western Montana, where all my generation spent more time in what were then called Card and Billiard Parlors than in school or at home. In the early part of this century the Card and Billiard Emporium was "the home away from home," and home was only where we ate and slept. Usually, the first table was the billiard table, because in Montana billiards was thought of as the sport of the upper class and was played only by the town's best barbers and the one vice-president of the bank. Then came three pool tables with dead cushions and concrete balls that hairy loggers hit so hard they jumped off the tables. At the rear, enthroned by several steps as at the Quadrangle Club, was the card room, in the center of which was the poker table under an enormous green shade. In the glare of the circle of light were always two or three poker players trying to look clumsy. They were housemen or "shills" waiting for some lumberjack to drop by who had just cashed his summer's check. If you were any good at cards yourself, you could see it was hard work for them to look clumsy.

We high school players were pool players, although we should like to have been billiard players if for no other reason than that each billiard player was so elite he had a woman besides a wife, but we could rarely finance our aspirations. It cost twenty-five cents an hour to play billiards, and only ten cents a game for rotation pool and, as any high school rotation-pool player knows, it is no great trick, when the houseman is not looking, to sneak balls back on the table that have already been sunk and thus to prolong the game.

When I came to the University as a Graduate Assistant then, I was just as good a billiard player as I had had spare twenty-five cent pieces when I was in high school, and still aspiring to be better, I ate my lunch early to get downstairs and watch the club champion.

Michelson was the best billiard player I have ever seen at the

University, and I think I have seen all the really good ones, including the barbers at the Reynolds Club. At first I was somewhat embarrassed to see how good he was, because I did not expect to find any academic type as good at a "man's sport" as the best we had in western Montana. But the more I thought about it and the more I learned about Michelson, the less surprised I became. Before long, I comforted myself with the question, "Why not? He's the best head-and-hands man in the world."

So it wasn't just billiards I watched when I arrived early every noon to watch Michelson play billiards. I came to watch his hands. The year 1928 was still in an age which counted men who made machines among its marvels and took for granted that the rest of men could use tools and that women could embroider beautifully. Edison still performed his wonders, but the wonders of Bell and Edison were more or less household utilities. Michelson's head-and-hands made machines almost godlike in properties, designed to tell us how it was with the universe. His favorite creation was his interferometer, with which, among other things, he (and later his collaborator, Edward Morley) had performed an experiment that shook the old universe and gave Einstein a big push toward creating a new one with his theory of relativity.

Before the Michelson-Morley experiment, the common scientific assumption was that the universe consisted of bodies of matter moving through and permeated by a substance that, although invisible, had somehow itself to be material. This substance at first was spelled "aether." Since Michelson tended to believe that the major theories of the universe were already in and that accordingly the chief jobs left to do were to measure what was sailing around in the ether, his head and hands produced his interferometer which split a light wave, sending one half with the orbit of the earth and back again where it met the other half wave length that had been sent on a return trip at right angles to the orbit of the earth. If there were ether out there (unless it were being carried along by the earth as if it were an envelope of the earth), the expectation was that when the two halves of the light wave rejoined they would be "out of phase," since one had held a course parallel to "the ether drift" and the other had crossed it at right angles and returned. The difference between the two half-light waves would indeed be small, but Michelson was sure he could measure it—and measure it he did, again and again—only to conclude reluctantly that there was no difference and that therefore there was no stationary ether "out there" and that light traveled at equal velocity in all directions.

In 1928 we only crudely knew how these negative results of the Michelson-Morley experiment opened the universe to Einstein's theories of relativity and we had even vaguer notions of the kind of machine that left Newtonian physics lying in a heap feebly struggling to get out from under its own ruins.

I had heard, however, something about the interferometer, and, having worked ten or eleven summers in the Forest Service and logging camps, I had enough feeling for tools to make it hard for me to keep my mind solely on billiards. After Michelson would run ten or twelve billiards with a touch so delicate that the three balls could always be covered by a hat, I found myself wondering how he had ever made a machine so delicate its finding would be invalid if it vibrated half a wave length of light, a whole wave length of light being so small that it can't be seen by our most powerful microscope. A fancy, wide-angle billiard would also take my mind off the game, because I knew just from the nature of the experiment that the machine had to turn ninety degrees without vibration (in mercury, I later found) so that any change in the pattern of the light waves could be observed. Perhaps the most American, air-conditioned question I kept asking was, "How the hell in the 1880s did he ever keep the machine in a temperature that probably couldn't vary a tenth of a degree?"

You don't have to have a diagram of the interferometer to realize why it was Michelson's favorite creation or why Michelson must have felt about his interferometer something of the way Galileo felt about his telescope:

"O telescope, instrument of much knowledge, more precious than any sceptre! Is not he who holds thee in his hand made king and lord of the works of God?"

But even this poetical outpouring isn't as moving a tribute to a machine as the factual statement about the interferometer made by Arthur Stanley Eddington, the English astronomer; it is a machine, he said, that can detect "a lag of one-ten-thousand-billionth of a second in the arrival of a light wave."

A master's hands

No wonder that before long the astronomers tried to enlist Michelson's hands in their service and succeeded. Dissatisfied with their own attempts, they urged him to give them the first accurate measurement of a star. For the first star ever to have its diameter measured accurately he picked a big one with a big name a long way off—Betelgeuse, linear diameter 240,000,000 miles (2,300 times larger than our sun) and 150 light years from the earth.

His hands were legendary long before I ever saw them. As legend, they were part fact and some fiction. For instance, I soon heard he was a fine violinist and a mini-Stradivarius who made his own beautiful instruments, but I think the truth is that, while his Jewish father was out selling pick-handles to California gold miners, his Polish mother kept him indoors to "practice, practice, practice," with the result that he became a fine violinist and, in his turn, spent half an hour before going to his lab in passing on his love and skill to his daughters. The business, though, about his making violins was just a fictional tribute to his hands.

It is a fact, however, that at the end of his first year at Annapolis he stood at the top of his class in drawing and that all his life he expressed himself by sketches and watercolors. Often in late afternoons if you looked over the wall in front of his beautiful home at 1220 East 58th Street (just behind the Robie House) you could see him in the sunshine and shadow of his yard painting shadow and sunshine.

Many of his last late afternoons in Chicago he spent either in his yard or at the Quadrangle Club. In those days, before so much of the Quadrangle Club was turned into an eating place, there was a beautiful chess room on the second floor, and on late afternoons his slightly stooped shoulders were often reflected in the dark and light squares of ingrained wood. He had been good enough once to play the American chess champion, Frank James Marshall, who however was not overpowered by his unorthodox openings, as most of his opponents were, and is supposed to have remarked that the physicist's game was a little long on imagination and passion.

He also had the reputation of having been a very good tennis player, but I have no memory of ever seeing him play; perhaps at seventy-five he had quit the game, but supposedly he had been very good.

It may not be so surprising as it first seems that he was not a good bridge player, although always wanting to be in the game. It is hard to predict just where there is going to be a gap in somebody's genetic tape, and, before I ever heard the word "genetic," I was learning in the Quadrangle Club that a gene can be very narrow and not include what seems almost necessarily a part of it. For instance, Leonard Eugene Dickson, the outstanding mathematician, who at the time was writing his classic works on the theory of numbers, was sometimes a poor card player. Anton J. Carlson was also not a good bridge player, although he was nationally famous as an exponent of the scientific method in the biological sciences ("Vat iss da evidence?"). In fact, there were quite a few card players in western Montana who would have taken the money from the world-famous intellectuals who gathered at noon in the card room of the Quadrangle Club in those days (and since).

After watching Michelson play bridge for a while, you could predict more or less the kind of mistake he would make, and it was not unrelated to the American champion's description of his chess game. He would make a bid short of game, but, after getting the bid, would see that, if he took and made two long finesses, he could come in with a little slam. Of course, a little slam would make only a few points difference since he hadn't bid it, but he would take the two finesses and not only lose both but lose his bid on an absolutely "lay-down hand." He was a rather small man, as you know, and he would look with almost childlike incredulity at the ruined remains of his daring invention of two long finesses where none was a sure thing.

There may also have been a causal relation between his shortcomings in bridge and chess. As the great head-and-hands scientist, the games that he was really good at involved great skill with a cue, a violin bow, a paint brush or a racket, but chess and bridge required no gift of hands. This is just a guess. The University of Chicago had as yet no Nobel Prize winners by the names of George Wells Beadle and James Dewey Watson to decode the hodge-podge of genetic tape that makes us one, or to explain why Michelson, who when it came to games was a mini-Leonardo da Vinci, with a wide spread of gifts, was not wanted as a bridge partner. It is easier to understand Carlson's case—we certainly don't think of there being much connection between animal experimentation and fifty-two cards and two jokers—and there wasn't.

Dickson, the master of numbers, was sometimes expectedly brilliant in a game where only 13 x 4 numbers were involved; his habitual troubles were at least partly environmental—he had come here by way of Texas. He almost consistently overbid and, when he lost three or four hands in a row, he would slam his cards down on the table and leave the card room in a rage, always denouncing Carlson on the way out. No matter who had misplayed—Carlson, Michelson, or himself—he always denounced Carlson. While the cards were still shivering on the table, he would shout, "Why the hell, Carlson, don't you go back to your lab and feed your dogs? And don't let Irene Castle catch you killing any of them."

Overbidding three or four hands in a row and then blaming the great biologist seemed to put the great mathematician in the right state of mind to race back to his office and resume his classic studies on the theory of numbers.

But be sure that Dickson or no one else ever even mentioned that Michelson did not play bridge well. Michelson was something like the other great University tradition we had in those days (observed in these present days only by James Cate and me)—namely, that the University shield in the floor of the Reynolds Club, in front of the entrance to the cafeteria, should never be stepped on. No one wanted to play with Michelson, but he was Michelson, and no one ever stepped on him and said he did not play bridge well.

At seventy-five, though, he was still the best billiard player in the club. He even looked like a billiard player. In fact, he looked like everything he did well—he looked like a violinist, a water colorist, a chess player and a physicist. And he still looked like an Annapolis-trained naval officer. At seventy-five, he was slight, trim, and handsome. He was quietly dressed, with a high, stiff collar and a small, sharp mustache. He was small all over, and even his hands did not look particularly unusual. In fact, one of the fascinations of his hands was that they looked fairly ordinary. I suppose we are used to thinking of a master's hands as being long and powerful and "esthetic," but the hands of the greatest of all billiard players, Willie Hoppe, were not particularly unusual just to look at, although those of his great rival, Jake Shaefer (the Younger), conformed to the picture in our minds and were like long and powerful bridges. I had learned, though, while working in logging camps, that a man's hands don't always tell how good he is with them.

Michelson was slightly stooped-shouldered (possibly from age), and his small size and slight stoop made him fit the proportions of a billiard table when he was taking a shot, and, when he was standing, he looked as if he were leaning over his cue to chalk it. With a shift of context, of course, the slight stoop and quiet elegance made him look like a violinist, a painter and a chess player.

Like most of the very good "downtown players" at Bensinger's, he seemed to shoot slowly, an obvious illusion if you kept track of the number of points he was making. It would be more accurate, therefore, to say he shot steadily and rhythmically, only occasionally taking more time to study one shot than another. Those who had seen him shoot in his prime said he was best at three-cushion billiards and credited his skill at this wide-angle game to his mastery of physics, but when I saw him play, his long game was his weakness, possibly because his eyesight was not so sharp as it had been.

In 1928 what he was best at was getting the three balls close together and then "nursing" them—that is, making long runs by keeping the balls together with a soft, delicate stroke. When they slowly worked apart, he would bring them together again with a "position shot" that required an understanding of the angle each ball would take when it came off a cushion, together with perfect control of the speed and hence the distance each ball would travel. Speed and angles he had under his control. When I saw him play, he was essentially a control player.

It would be non-scientific to describe him as a great billiard player but he was a very good amateur player. At seventy-five he could have played downtown at Bensinger's, and he was the best billiard player in the history of the University. I saw him run over forty several times, and it was not unusual for him to put a string together of twenty or thirty; he had to start with a tough "leave" if he didn't make five or ten.

Once he handed me his cue and said, "Shoot a few yourself." Considering my general confusion, I thought I did pretty well. In fact, he said, "Not bad." Then he added, "But you use 'English' on too many of your shots." English comes from putting a spin on the cue-ball by hitting it on one side instead of the center so that it comes off the cushion or another ball at an unusual angle. "Once in a while it is necessary to use English," he said, "but it is hard to predict accurately. Cue your ball in the center as often as you can. Don't use something hard to control unless you have to."

Only this once did he hand me his cue and ask me to shoot, so once must have satisfied him that, although I wasn't good enough to play with him, he could turn to me now and then and lift an eyebrow.

Often when he missed a shot, he stood silently studying the green cloth until (I think) he had reconstructed the preceding series of shots and had decided where he had started to lose control of the balls. Once he said when he missed a shot, "I am getting old."

Just he and I were present, so he said this to me or himself, but I had to let him know I heard it and I have always been glad I did. I said, "No, no. It was a hard shot, but it was the one you should have taken, and you barely missed it."

"Are you sure?" he asked.

I said, "I am sure. The easy shot would have left the balls spread all over the table. Any of the good players down at Bensinger's would have played it the way you did, and a lot of them would have missed.''

Extended epigram

I think that he was glad I had stopped him from blaming old age, but he was through for the day. He locked his cue into the rack on the wall, and said, either to me or himself or the wall, ''Billiards is a good game.''

He made sure that his tie was in the center of his stiff collar before he added, ''But billiards is not as good a game as painting.''

He rolled down his sleeves and put on his coat. Elegant as he was, he was a workman and took off his coat and rolled up his sleeves when he played billiards. As he stood on the first step between the billiard room and the card room, he added, ''But painting is not as good a game as music.''

On the next and top step, he concluded, ''But then music is not as good a game as physics.''

As you can see, I have never forgotten this extended epigram, but for many years I thought of it largely as an extended epigram and for some time I thought probably he had shaped it for me, knowing vaguely that I was in English and should appreciate a literary construction that extended across the billiard room to the top of the stairs. As I grew older and more detached from myself, however, I could see nothing in our relations that would have suggested to him what I intended to do with my life, so next I came to assume that it was just a stylish remark he made to himself, because at seventy-five he was still very stylish—in appearance, dress, serenity, and slowness of movement that turned out not to be slowness but the shortest distance between two points, which is one definition of grace.

Always, though, I must have sensed that this extended epigram was more than a reflection of style, because, forty-five years later, by which time I had several subjects I might have talked about, I suddenly decided I would tell the Alumni Cabinet about Michelson's comment on games. I also decided it was time for me to clarify to myself what was missing to me but I always knew was there, so I went over to the President's Archives, got Michelson's file and read his most serious scientific prose. Then, not long afterwards— but unfortunately not until after I gave my talk to the Alumni Cabinet—I discovered and read the humanly and scientifically perceptive biography of him by his youngest daughter. You should read it, too, if you wish to experience for a short time Michelson's universe which moves in beauty playing games. It is not a universe governed by morality or theology but by esthetics, mechanics, and gamesmanship, all shades of one another.

In 1928, then, Michelson was not talking to the wall when he said, after missing a correct but hard shot: "Billiards is a good game, but billiards is not as good a game as painting, but painting is not as good a game as music, but then music is not as good a game as physics."

He was saying much the same thing many years earlier, only more formally, and more beautifully. In 1899, for instance, he began the Lowell Lectures on physics before his Boston audience by speaking first of esthetics:

> If a poet could at the same time be a physicist, he might convey to others the pleasure, the satisfaction, almost the reverence, which the subject inspires. The esthetic side of the subject is, I confess, by no means the least attractive to me. Especially is its fascination felt in the branch which deals with light, and I hope the day may be near when a Ruskin will be found equal to the description of the beauties of coloring, the exquisite graduations of light and shade, and the intricate wonders of symmetrical forms and combinations of forms which are encountered at every turn.

In the games that were going on in the universe, the participants were not only the universe and those hoping to understand it, but even the machines that were made to help the understanding. Of one of his machines that Michelson could never quite master, he said:

> One comes to regard the machine as having a personality—I had almost said a feminine personality—requiring humoring, coaxing, cajoling—even threatening! But finally one realizes that the personality is that of an alert and skillful player in an intricate but fascinating game—who will take immediate advantage of the mistakes of his opponent, who "springs" the most disconcerting surprises, who never leaves any result to chance—but who nevertheless plays fair—in strict accordance with the rules of the game. These rules he knows and makes no allowance if you do not. When *you* learn them and play accordingly, the game progresses as it should.

Einstein left behind, not only a formulation of the universe, but a formulation of Michelson's delight in it. His telegram on the one-hundredth anniversary of Michelson's birthday began:

> I always think of Michelson as the artist in Science. His greatest joy seemed to come from the beauty of the experiment itself, and the elegance of the method employed.

Although I watched Michelson play billiards regularly at noon for a few months before he retired from the University, I have the feeling now that he never came to know anything about me, except that I put English on too many of my shots and so did not have perfect control of them.

But I am certain that eventually I came to know something important about him, perhaps in part because I taught literature, and certainly in part because I was brought up in pool halls and logging camps—he was an artist and played many games well, especially those involving something like a cue, a brush, a bow, or, best of all, a box with slits and silvered mirrors. In that game he was playing with light and a star.

WORKS CITED

Livingston, Dorothy M. *The Master of Light: A Biography of Albert A. Michelson.* New York: Charles Scribner's Sons, 1973.

'This Quarter I Am Taking McKeon': A Few Remarks on the Art of Teaching

Norman Maclean*

*　*　*

It has been predetermined that I should talk today on the impossible subject, teaching, in almost impossible circumstances. Anyone here could and probably should get up and give this talk, and all of us would say fundamentally the same few things, even if somewhat differently.

For instance, I am sure that any of us would start off by saying that he never read or heard anything that helped him much with his own teaching. I am retired now, and in looking back I can think of only one such thing that helped me, and I'm not sure it helped, but I admit using it.

I started teaching at Dartmouth College immediately after my graduation there, and, also immediately, one of my classes was inspected by a senior member of the faculty. The same thing was done to one of my classes when I started teaching here, but here instead of saying they were "inspecting" my class they said they

*" 'This Quarter I Am Taking McKeon': A Few Remarks on the Art of Teaching" by Norman Maclean is excerpted from *The University of Chicago Magazine* 66 (January/February 1974), pp. 8–12. Copyright © 1974 by *The University of Chicago Magazine*. Reprinted by permission of the publisher.

were visiting, and sent a woman. But at Dartmouth they sent a man. His name was McCallum and he was tall, red-headed and Scotch, with a long sardonic moustache. He would have resembled Mephistopheles, if Mephistopheles had been Scotch, as he well might have been.

Like most Scotchmen, he took religion very seriously, only he happened to be an atheist, and would not allow the word God to be mentioned in his classes. He was the first great teacher I ever had, but naturally my feelings were mixed about being inspected by someone who did not think very much even of God. Still, I regarded him so highly as a teacher that I was sure he would tell me something about teaching when my class was over that, however harsh, would let me in on the secret to the mystery.

I discovered later that he himself had had no mixed feelings about the coming prospect. He thought the whole business was beneath him—and beneath me, for that matter. But it was some years later when I found out these feelings. In the meantime some hours had passed after he inspected my class and he hadn't called me into his office; and then some days, and finally several weeks.

At times in life unexpected silence is a momentary relief, but it can go on until you can't bear it any longer and finally you have to hear something, no matter what. So finally I made an appointment with him at his office and when I came in he asked, "Yes?" as if he didn't know why I came. I couldn't think of any way to approach the subject gradually, so I asked, "What did you think of the class?" And he asked, "What class?" I said, "My class, the one you inspected." Then he said, "It was all right." We had suddenly run out of conversation, but still I couldn't leave. I was still hoping for the secret that would clear up the life that was to come. Finally I asked, "Don't you have something to tell me that would help me be a good teacher?"

Sartorial pedagogy

He thought for a while and then said, "Wear a different suit every day of the week." He had come from Princeton.

I said, "I can't afford that."

"Well, then," he said, "wear a different necktie."

I had been brought up to believe that you made the most in life of what little you had, and, since this is all that has ever been told me about my teaching, I must confess that I wore a different necktie every day of the week until I retired. I never did get up into the daily suit class.

So, as we all know, teaching is something like physics or music. It is mostly biological. It is something you can do—or not do—when you are fairly young. If you can do it, experience will make you a little better. Then toward retirement you will get a little worse. I have just given a complete log of a teacher. I feel that I have slipped now to where I am about as good as when I started teaching at twenty. In between, there were times when I was a little better. That's it.

If, though, I have heard only one thing that has been directly useful to me as a teacher, I have had the opportunity to watch unusually gifted teachers through the years. I don't know whether this results in anything one can incorporate directly into his own teaching, teaching being such a highly individualized art, but it does make one a better teacher by lifting up the spirit and making one feel elevated about what he has chosen to do in life. Though I retired after teaching in only two colleges, Dartmouth and here, they are two colleges that put great premium upon fine teaching. When I went as a student to Dartmouth in 1920, I was told that a great tradition had only recently died and might at any moment be revived. The tradition was called "horning." Presumably Dartmouth students for generations had rented a barn and stored hundreds of horns in it, and when a teacher was hired who was something less than pleasing, the students would assemble at night at the barn, arm themselves with horns and march around the teacher's house, for all practical purposes terminating his contract irrespective of whether, according to the American Association of University Professors, the contract still had three years to go.

In later years, I came to doubt whether in fact there had ever been such a custom, because when I was a junior I acquired a couple of teachers who I thought might be improved by musical accompaniment, but the barn where the horns were stored could not be found, either in daylight or literally by lantern. But even if it was only a legend, it worked. I even came to suspect it was a legend started and nurtured by the administration, as an effective and cheap device to get some very creative teaching.

At the University of Chicago, of course, one of our chief devices to spur the teacher on to higher effort is the Quantrell Award for Excellence in Undergraduate Teaching. It has also proved to be a very effective device for encouraging teachers to put forth their best efforts, but it is more costly than the Dartmouth method. Whereas the Dartmouth method works by trepidation and musical chairs and mythical horns, the University of Chicago method works by showers of solid blessings amounting to four and sometimes five awards each year of $1,000 each. Although admittedly the Dartmouth method of improving pedagogy was effective, I am sure that those of us who have received the $1,000 tax exempt award think of the University of Chicago's method as the more humane.

*   *   *

Partly since the two universities where I have taught have had very different but very effective extracurricular stimuli to get the maximum yardage out of their teachers, I have had the privilege of observing some remarkable teaching in my time, a good deal of it done by some present today.

For some years after I started out on my observation tours I saw nothing in common between one great teacher and another. For instance, Wayne Booth, who gave us this morning one of the few fine convocation speeches I have ever heard, walks into his classroom, takes off his coat, hangs it on the back of the chair, sits on the corner of his desk, which he uses as a launching pad.

But his great master—and mine, too, for that matter—was R. S. Crane, and he couldn't have been more formal. He wore a tall starched collar and I can still see the tip of his gold collar button only partially hidden under the knot of his tie.

Joe Schwab punches a student all over the ring until he finally gets him in a corner and disposes of him. So Joe Schwab teaches like a prize fighter.

But Tom Hutchinson taught like an architect. He began his lectures just as the bell rang and his last word came just as it rang again and, when you looked back over it, all the parts were there in just the right order and size, and it had the beauty that comes from something built in serenity.

So you can teach like a prize fighter and be a great teacher, or you can teach like an architect and be a great teacher, or you can be a great teacher in shirt sleeves or in back of a gold collar button. It seems you can do about anything and be a great teacher.

But if you like to go around watching great teachers, as I used to when I could sit longer in one place than I can now, you will eventually see certain common characteristics emerging amid all the variety of gymnastic techniques. And, on the basis of some of the more obvious of these common characteristics, I am willing to make a rough description of a great teacher just to get started on this part of the subject. Later I hope to refine it, but I'll start by saying that a great teacher is a tough guy who cares deeply about something that is hard to understand.

To vivify what I have just said, I think I'll take one of the most popular and flamboyant of undergraduate teachers in our College's history. I take him in deference to Mr. Bate, whose honorary degree was awarded today in part because he is one of the world's most renowned scholars and teachers of early 19th century Romanticism.

Teddy Linn of long ago had no such distinction as a scholar, but what he lacked in scholarship about Romanticism he made up in being a flamboyant version of Romanticism itself. It was forty-five years ago this autumn when I went to observe his opening class in his favorite course in the English Romantic poets, and I remember the class as if it had been held yesterday. Well, I don't remember the first few minutes of the class, because those of us who hadn't seen him in action before were worried that the cigarette on the edge of his lip would burn his lip in another half-inch, but the cigarette evidently always went out in another quarter of an inch and stuck there the rest of the hour.

Mr. Linn, in his introduction to Romanticism, mentioned no such aged and agricultural figures as Wordsworth, and he said nothing on the opening day about Coleridge and German metaphysics, although Coleridge and Wordsworth came first chronologically. For his opening words, he jumped the first generation of English Romantic poets and went straight for Keats.

Keats was dead, he said, when he was no older than some of them in the class and only a few years older than most of them. He was immortal at an age when they did well to get C plus on a theme in English composition because it had no split infinitives or dangling participles. He said that despite this notable difference, they and Keats were one in that Keats gave the finest expression in all literature of what was best in them. He said when you grew older, as he had, you grew used to things, but youth trembled at the beauty of the earth, even when death stood close by. And he said Keats knew he was dying, and he recited the "Ode to Melancholy" and repeated the final stanza which begins

> She dwells with Beauty—Beauty that must die;
> And Joy, whose hand is ever at his lips
> Bidding adieu.

Then he told them a story, somewhat apocryphal, I am sure, but so spiritually true that I—and I am sure the rest of the class—will never forget it. He told them how Keats had been sent to Rome when it was discovered he was dying of tuberculosis, and how an art student friend of his by the name of Severn nursed him in his last illness. And how one day Severn had gone out shopping, and when he came back he found Keats leaning on his elbow staring at his pillow. And when Severn got closer to the bed he saw that Keats had hemorrhaged while he had been gone and so was staring at his life blood. Then suddenly Keats either saw or felt that Severn was present, and raised his head, and said, "Look, man, at that red against that white."

"And so," Mr. Linn said, "you will bring in a paper tomorrow on John Keats." There was a long silence, and I am sure Mr. Linn knew how it was going to be broken. Finally, a fraternity pledge raised his hand and asked, ''Did you say that paper is due tomorrow?''

''That's right,'' Mr. Linn said. ''Tomorrow. That's just to let you know what big teeth your grandmother has.''

Everybody in class had his paper in the next day, and, although I never saw any of them, it's a good bet that none of them was much good. But that wasn't the idea.

I used this incident to illustrate my rough definition before discussing it, especially the ingredients of being tough and caring deeply.

When I say ''tough,'' I realize we are in an age when students seem to be demanding that teachers stroke the silk on their egos while serving them sherry with the other hand, and I have one favorable thing to say about all this—the students don't seem to care whether the sherry is good or not, and after a while they tire of the whole business.

The truth is, no matter what students seem to be saying at the moment, they want things tough, too. A student has to be sick to want a teacher for a pal or a pet. Of course, students don't care to be roughed up just to give somebody else pleasure, and by being tough I don't mean being rude or unsympathetic, although I want to make clear that I do not feel any compunction about being courteous to all people at all times, either in a classroom or anywhere else. You treat students the way you treat other people—the way you think they deserve to be treated.

I would be glad to argue this matter psychologically or even philosophically. Outside, just ahead of the student is the world of lumps-and-bumps. Is day-care what he needs most at this stage of the game to help him be ready? And, if so, just where did we acquire the breast-development to give it to him? But I am not really looking for arguments today. I have included ''toughness'' in the definition of great teachers because, on observation, I have found it one of their few common characteristics.

Some years ago I had a student by the name of Liz Ginsburg. She was a great handsome, intelligent girl who remains one of my all-time favorites. I hadn't seen her for some time, so when I ran into her I asked, "Liz, what are you doing this quarter?" And she looked at me a little glassy-eyed and said, "This quarter I am taking McKeon," which, as all of us know who have been students of his, is just a refined way of saying, "This quarter McKeon is taking me."

What a great compliment for a great and tough teacher! Would that the campus were alive with large, handsome intelligent girls murmuring, "This quarter I am taking Maclean."

Then I also want to say a little about the part of the definition that has to do with caring deeply about something hard to understand. This is the part without which there is nothing. In this student-oriented age when we are all huddled together with "togetherness," I should like to step slightly apart and say I have seen great teachers who didn't care much about students, including America's first Nobel Prize winner, Albert Abraham Michelson.

There was another eminent scientist who by legend found teaching very disturbing because, as he said, "Every time I remember the name of a student I forget the name of a fish." But, according to the legend, he was also a fine teacher, and, if the account is true, he became the first president of Stanford.

Most teachers like some students for some reason or other, and the reverse is true—most students have a few teachers they like, sometimes for very obscure reasons. But, in the legend, our scientific president of Stanford was a fine teacher because he liked fish, and you can't be one unless you do. And in addition have, as you can see he had, the power of conveying his feelings about fish.

On the other hand, I don't want to push a teacher to a place where he has to publish or perish. After all, if it had not been for students of his, Socrates would have had no bibliography. Perhaps that is why he didn't get tenure. If one becomes contemporary and looks at the list of Quantrell award winners in a disinterested way, he finds that of the 127, perhaps half also have the distinction as scholars. The count could vary five or ten one way or the other, depending upon how one feels about friendship while he is counting, but that roughly is the proportion, and it is roughly the proportion

I have seen to exist among the great university teachers I have observed in something over half a century of counting.

Teachers' genes

It is for my half of this proportion that I should like to say a few words. But just to get the cards dealt fairly before we begin this game, let me add that, during the same half century of observation, something less than half of the great scholars have *not* been great teachers, or even very good ones, a fact which has left the world somewhat short of very good teachers.

Now, as to the particular fraction for which I was going to speak. First of all, we believe that scholarship should and does pervade this university and other great universities. Secondly, we think that in some fundamental senses we are scholars, but, for this to be true, scholarship has to exist in several fundamental senses besides the conventional one that results in a long bibliography.

No matter how we think of scholarship, we must at least think of it as the discovery of truth, and in the conventional sense this discovery should also be a discovery of some significance to our colleagues. It is in this sense that we say that a great university is known for its great scholars and that a person is—if he is—a great scholar and a great teacher.

But a teacher must have a wider range of discovery than this. A teacher must forever be making discoveries to himself—he must have a gene marked "Freshness of the World."

And then he must have another gene that gives him the power to lead students to making discoveries—ultimately, he hopes, to the power of self-discovery. This gene might be marked, "You-Don't-Say-So?" However, many of these stirring discoveries may have been made, indeed should have been made, before by other men and women, and hence are not publishable in a scholarly journal.

Now there is this third gene marked, "The Best and Freshest on the Subject." As a minimum, the great teacher must have a half of this gene—the half that gives him command of the best that is known among his colleagues. However, he may or may not have the other half of the gene which leads him as a minimum to a hankering after immortality in a footnote.

I should like to leave this part of the subject in language that does not echo the "publish or perish" controversy, and so I shall say that the great teacher should care as much as any man for his subject and be able to convey his pleasure in it far better than most.

Perhaps a Freudian way could be found to describe the great teacher that would at least be more interesting than measuring the length of his bibliography. There is no greater commonplace from Freud than that in the beginning we are all Id, the principle of pleasure and lust, and the Ego, the principle of reason and sanity, comes later and is only a feeble outgrowth of the Id, is always subservient to it, and is developed only to protect the Id from the censure of society and to allow it the maximum fulfillment in a world where orgy is a bad word.

But long before I reached the age of retirement I realized the reverse of this can be a second truth. The ego can become so powerful that it can woo the id and make pleasure a servant of reason and sanity. The reason can become so powerful and fancy that it can make love to the id and say, "Look at me. Feel my muscles and see how graceful and beautiful I am. As for gifts, I can bring you samples of the moon. Forget about women's lib and come along and pledge to love, honor and obey me, and consider yourself lucky." I would be willing, then, I think, to consider the art of teaching as the art of perverting nature, as nature is given to us by St. Sigmund, and I would accept, not wholeheartedly I admit, a definition of teaching as the art of enticing the ego to seduce the id into its services.

My father, I am sure, however, would have had nothing to do with such a definition. As a Presbyterian minister, he would have remained aloof from any definition that began with seduction and ended with the id. What he would have said would have been something more or less like this: "Teaching is the art of conveying the delight that comes from an act of the spirit (and from here on the

Presbyterianism gets thicker), without ever giving anyone the notion that the delight comes easy.''

Although I realize the variety of religious experience present here today, I shall end on this Presbyterian note. So teaching will remain as the art of conveying the delight that comes from an act of the spirit, without ever giving anyone the notion that the delight comes easy.

But all I really know about teaching is that, to do it well, supposedly you should change your necktie every day of the week.

Montana Memory: Talk at the Institute of the Rockies

Norman Maclean*

* * *

A man has to have a lot of reasons for writing his first book after becoming 70, and at least a couple of them should be good in case at that age the book isn't. I have one I am sure is pretty good. Before I die and disintegrate altogether, I wanted to put some of the pieces of myself together, and I have some pretty big splits in my personality. We talk as if the problem of identity is a problem of youth—but we always have problems of trying to find out who we are, and life is very persistent in splitting us into pieces. Yet we all yearn—if I may use a theological phrase—to achieve some kind of unity of the soul somewhere along the way.

One major split in my personality is fairly easy to state but difficult to reconcile—on the one hand, I was brought up in western Montana, and from the time I was 16 I was working in the Forest Service and logging camps. On the other hand, since 1924 I have made my living teaching American and English literature in two

*"Montana Memory: Talk at the Institute of the Rockies" by Norman Maclean is reprinted from the text of the speech Norman Maclean delivered on April 4, 1977 in Billings, Montana. Copyright © 1977 by Norman Maclean.

fairly high-powered universities—Dartmouth and the University of Chicago—and ended my teaching career holding the professorship named after the founder and first president of the University of Chicago. So I wanted, before I died, to make one piece out of a once pretty good timber-willie and the William Rainey Harper Professor of English.

Those of you who are as old as I am can remember, and the rest of you can imagine, how beautiful Montana was at the beginning of this century—and our cabin was only 16 miles from the glaciers. And you can remember or can imagine the beauty of what men and women could do with their hands in the days when in the woods it was all done by hand or horse or foot.

In the half century I taught literature, I was largely given the freedom to teach the literature of my choice, so naturally I chose literature that I felt was beautiful. I have had the great fortune, then, of spending most of my life in the beauty of the woods and books.

So when I went about writing my first book, as you will see, I went back to my memory of Montana for my energy and to my years of teaching literature for the power lines to conduct it.

Perhaps none of us can define Montana Memory exactly, or would care to if we could, but we all know its reality and importance. You can't live in Montana without an extra amount of memory. I can't catch Cutthroat trout at the beginning of the summer until I can remember you can't set the hook quite so fast as you have to on Rainbow trout—and, of course, you can still get killed or at least into a lot of trouble if your memory fails you and you leave your rifle leaning against a tree quite a way from where you are skinning out a bear.

But given my book and the way I am spending my retirement, I naturally want to limit my consideration of Montana Memory to its relations to art. It is not hard to see why Montana Memory has been crucial to the art of Montana story-telling, past or present. It is an art practiced not only by such a great living professional as Alfred Guthrie; it is still an art spread widely among us who tell stories just for the hell of it, although we don't have many campfires any more to tell them around. We tell them now at weddings, funerals, and to our children. A couple of summers ago a dear friend of many of us was very sick in Helena, and many of us gathered around to wait. Among the many were Irvin Rieke, who owns the Piper agency here in Billings; Brian O'Connell, who used to own the great Rock Creek cattle ranch outside of Wolf Creek; and Frank Wiley, the old Miles City boy who wrote the history of aviation in Montana and had a great share in the making of it. For two days there was nothing to do but wait, and I never heard better Montana stories.

But when I was young—certainly no older than 17 or 18—I was telling Montana stories myself. There was a small bunch of us of the same age who would sit in the evening on the steps of the First National Bank in Missoula, then owned by the Jacobs family, and tell Montana stories. We were all young, but we all worked in the woods in the summer, and I don't think you can be a Montana story-teller unless you have worked in the woods or on ranches. We sat in the moonlight on the corner of Higgins and Front Streets and told stories until we were very late for our dates with our girls. This was a great experience for developing our narrative art although it made us all a little retarded in the art of making love.

The moonlight at the corner of Higgins and Front was also important. As an early ingredient in Montana stories, moonlight acts something like the early campfire. It helps to explain why there has to be a flickering magic in a Montana story. The first review of my book was in *Publishers Weekly* by the hard-nosed New York senior editor, Barbara Bannon, and I knew I had made it when she said, "Maclean takes his brother flyfishing on the Big Blackfoot and with his own offhand magic turns his memories into something unique and marvelous." It was not very "offhand magic"—it belongs to Montana stories and comes in good part from being told in moonlight or at campfires.

Montana Memory has its particular quality and magic, but, of course, it is also a species of Frontier Memory, the frontier, wherever it may be—the New England colonies, Mark Twain's Mississippi, Bret Harte's California, Willa Cather's Nebraska—all seemingly putting a great premium upon memory—memory just to survive from day to day and certainly memory to tell stories. It is not hard to think of four or five reasons why this is so. (1) The frontier world is full of adventures, and it draws adventurers for characters. Stories are happening all around—your plots and characters are almost made for you. (2) Often what is happening around you is also important historically. You are seeing history made and often are helping to make it. Mrs. Melloy, the wonderful head librarian of Montana's Historical Library, presides over a vast collection of Montana memories preserved as diaries and journals, some of the more famous being Langford's *Vigilante Days and Ways*, Granville Stuart's *Forty Years on the Frontier*, and Hanson's *The Conquest of the Missouri*. But nearly all Montana descendants have their private collection of family memoirs and albums. (3) On the frontier, the world in which your stories and histories happen is usually a beautiful world, perhaps a world of terror too but a highly scenic and memorable world. (4) On the frontier, you have to make most of your own pleasures. Each of you has to be his own radio station, creating his own amateur hour, and being able to turn a button and come on at the popular hours of eight and nine o'clock in the evening with Montana Memories.

Plato had a fancy theory that all knowledge was memory, but you don't have to be fancy to assert that on the frontier both survival and pleasure depend upon memory.

We need to remember Charley Russell to start thinking about Montana Memory as being a branch of Frontier Memory with its own shapes and colors. The world at large remembers Charley as a painter, but those of us who think we are Montana story-tellers all learned from his stories. We think in the art of the short, short story he was as good as Mark Twain, even though all his narrative classics are collected in one book, *Trails Plowed Under*.

But it is said he won many a pay-day story-telling contest when he was a cowboy, and I know a few of the stories supposedly with which he won this Triple A competition and perhaps should tape them for Mrs. Melloy's library and for posterity, even if they don't all advance the cause of purity and shining armor. Montana Memory was highly developed on pay-day when the cowhands came into town with their pay checks and told stories until they were broke, the one telling the best story having his booze and hotel bill paid.

Charley, of course, continued the development of his narrative art into his mature years. He painted in the mornings and, in the afternoons, crawled on his horse, went to the bar and swapped stories with his pals. It is said his wife, who ran his business affairs, allowed him to have just two dollars when he crawled onto his horse.

Charley's stories, of course, are built out of the main ingredients of Frontier Memory. (1) They are made out of high adventures and high adventurers—a cowpuncher riding his bucking horse over a cliff, both landing in the top of a tree, and the puncher calmly finishing rolling his cigarette while allowing himself to be cut out of the branches. (2) Sometimes they are at the other end of the spectrum of Frontier Memory, and are almost pure social history with no narrative or plot—perhaps an accurate and interesting account of the different kinds of saddles and spurs used on different parts of the range. Generally, however, there is a fusion of story and historical information. (3) And of course Charley's stories were told for pleasure, especially those that were told to pay his bar and hotel bills. Undoubtedly, among other things, the fact his stories come out of an oral tradition accounts in good part for their being very short stories. No matter who we are, we all have tried telling enough stories to know that not even our best friends will listen to one of our stories for more than ten minutes.

But I should like to point out at least one basic feature of Charley's stories that is a particular mark of Montana Memory—the basic emotional mixture pervading most of his stories and his paintings and drawings. I suppose that essentially the conventional Western tall tale is comic, and the comic spirit is certainly deep in Charley's art as it was in his view of life and as I hope it is in ours. But mixed with the comic and helping to separate his stories from the Western tall tale are sadness and pathos. Part of the sadness is tied up with his sense of history. He knew he had lived through one of America's great moments of history—he had lived to see all but the end. Listen to his title, *Trails Plowed Under*. It is a very powerful emotional combination—the comedy coming from the high adventures and joys experienced in the history we have seen. Comedy on the frontier can also be a quite opposite kind of thing—it can be a kind of bravery for meeting the dangers of the frontier and what lies ahead of us. Comedy is a Western way of playing down the big thing. The sadness is to see that what we have seen is about all over and from now on it is barb wire. Perhaps more important than Charley's memories of Montana is how he felt about these memories. They say a psychoanalyst has little notion of what our memories of our dreams mean unless we can remember how we felt about our dreams.

I'd like finally to talk for just a few minutes about my little book. It is a collection of stories told by someone who feels grateful for being exposed for long portions of his life to the beauty of the woods and the West and to the beauty of American and English literature.

They are also stories that try to combine, as Western stories often do, the pleasure of an interesting story with a historical record. They especially try to leave a record of how we did things in the world just before this one—the world of hand and horse and hand tools and horse tools. The history in these stories, then, is a kind of a history of hand craft, and the chief characters are experts with their hands—expert packers, expert sawyers, expert fishermen. . . . Like Western yarns, the stories at times also play with comedy because ultimately our lives do. But unlike Western yarns, they are essentially serious and go beyond Charley's sadness and pathos; some of them are ultimately tragic, again because life is—not merely Montana life but life. These qualities are all there and more besides—besides these qualities, I have already said the stories try to incorporate magic and beauty, because ultimately I have found these, also, in the life of Montana and in life itself.

I keep adding to the term "Montana life" the term "life itself," because, among other things, I think a weakness of Montana stories has been that they have been too local, too true of Montana only. Montana stories should be true of Montana and of the world beyond. My first story, "A River Runs Through It," is a tragedy— the tragedy of my brother who was one of the finest fishermen in the northwest, a reporter for the *Helena Independent*, a big gambler at Hot Springs, and who knows what else. He was a wonderful guy, but he saw to it that, much as he loved us, we never saw just what he was. He was a kind of hero to our father and to me, and yet we feared for him, but could not help him, in part because we didn't know what if anything he needed for help. In the end he was murdered, and in the end we do not know why. And in the end we do not know him and we do not know whether we could have helped him.

Paramount is asking for an option to put this story into film, and I have made it a requirement that they must not change it from a tragedy about someone you loved and did not understand and could not help. You don't have to come from Montana to understand that tragedy.

*   *   *

The Pure and the Good: On Baseball and Backpacking

Norman Maclean*

I must have been a little confused when I agreed to talk on this subject, "The Pure Good of Literature." A member of the Association of Departments of English (ADE) Executive Committee that planned the program, no less a person than Arthur Coffin, asked me whether I would as I was walking to the platform to talk to his students at Montana State University in Bozeman. "Pure" and "good" are words that don't come through to me clearly at normal altitudes, but Bozeman is such a beautiful town, with the Spanish Peaks behind it and the Bridger Mountains in front, that the pure and the good seem possible there, so I said yes, and went on to the platform to talk about something very different.

Next morning, though, I was troubled enough to look Arthur up before leaving the Gallatin Valley to ask whether I had heard him right, and he repeated himself in daylight and went on to say that maybe I didn't know but since I had retired from teaching there had been a steady decline in the enrollment of students in English.

*"The Pure and the Good: On Baseball and Backpacking" by Norman Maclean is reprinted from *Associations of Departments of English Bulletin* 61 (May 1979), pp. 3–5. Copyright © 1979 by Norman Maclean. Reprinted with permission of the publisher.

He stated this in such a way as to suggest some relation of cause and effect, so I remained sufficiently confused to be here this morning to speak, in New York of all places, about the pure and the good.

There isn't a chance, though, I will say anything timely to affect the job market. I began teaching in 1928 during the Great Boom but just before the Great Depression and, although I always had a job during the Depression, I never once in all those years got a raise in rank or salary. So I have taught in good times and bad times, without greatly affecting the economy.

Something tells me that this may be true of many of us. All we can do at any given time is to teach what we see as best in literature and, I may add, in ourselves. It is also true, however, that in literature, as in life, we may come to take things for granted when times are good, or may do the opposite—through affluence, get fancy and lose sight of the fundamentals in a sea of aesthetics. In either event, it probably makes sense to take a fresh look at ourselves when things are not good to be sure we are at our best.

For instance, it pays from time to time to see whether, as teachers, scholars, and critics of literature, we are as good as professional baseball writers or even as baseball fans. Baseball fans are among our leading exponents of the art-for-art's-sake school of criticism— to them the art of baseball is a thing in itself and sufficient unto itself. They love it deeply and are very learned about it. The difference between a double steal and a delayed steal is primer stuff to them, and, as critics, they all know it is a disfigurement of the art to try a steal of any kind when your team is three or four runs behind. They know what they are talking about, and they are willing to stand up all night to get a ticket to see the big game. I have just written a small book of stories that was widely enough reviewed to entitle me to the opinion that a fair number of professional literary critics don't even know what kinds of questions to ask about a book. There are people in the grandstands of our profession who wouldn't be allowed in the bleachers of baseball. And many of our students in poetry can't tell an anapest from third base.

I am old-fashioned. I believe that one must know something about craftsmanship to come to know and love an art in its purity. We just must assume that one of our greatest loves is of the things men and women make with their hands and hearts and heads. We must assume that some of these beautiful things are hard to make and that therefore it will probably be hard to know as much as we should about an art in order to love it as we should. Even the ordinary baseball fan operates on these assumptions.

But many of our students in poetry courses—even in graduate courses—can do nothing, for instance, with the rhythm of poems. Reading a poem to them is like going to the senior prom and not being able to dance. But they have to know some things about craft before they can see and feel some of the complex beauty that has given immortality to such a seemingly simple old ballad as "Lord Randal." To see its beauty they must see that part of it is in its complex rhythm and in the suitability of its rhythm to a musical form such as the ballad, and in particular to "Lord Randal." At the end, they should be able to write a paper showing that it has at least three rhythms superimposed on its base English accentual rhythm of falling-rising syllables—carefully varied iambs and anapests—as "o where hae ye been, Lord Randal, my son." But they should be able to go on from there and show that the music only begins with qualitative rhythm, that quantitative rhythm is concurrent with the qualitative, that above the patterned syllables are larger verbal units of half lines and whole lines falling into patterns, as in Hebrew verse, and that the four-line stanza itself eventually becomes a foot, with the first two lines being a question and the last two lines the answer. This patterned repetition of grammatical structure we might call grammatical rhythm, and with it comes another kind of rhythm, a patterned recurrence of pitch or key, the question asked in the first two lines by the anxious mother in a high female key and the answer in the last two lines in the low masculine tones of her dying son.

So in this old-time immortal ballad there are at least four rhythms harmonizing with one another: the qualitative patterned recurrence of stressed syllables; the quantitative rhythm of recurring half lines, whole lines, and four-line stanzas; the repeated grammatical structures within these quantitative units; and finally a patterned change of key within each stanza from high key in the first two lines to low key in the last two.

> "O where hae ye been, Lord Randal, my son?
>   O where hae ye been, my handsome young man?"
> "I hae been to the wild wood; mother, make my bed soon,
>   For I'm weary wi' hunting, and fain wald lie down."
>
> "Where gat ye your dinner, Lord Randal, my son?
>   Where gat ye your dinner, my handsome young man?"
> "I din'd wi' my true-love; mother, make my bed soon,
>   For I'm weary wi' hunting, and fain wald lie down."

Such a lovely old poem, forever fresh and forever carrying with it its own musical accompaniment.

Let us leave the baseball fans behind in the bleachers. Ultimately, of course, literature does not play a game unless it is the game of life, and life is impure—it flops around and has spasms and in between it runs too straight, routinized by jobs and families and what the neighbors think. What then can be pure or good about it?

From here on I speak for myself, while hoping I speak for others. As I look back at my life now that I have been allowed to pass considerably beyond my biblical allotment of three score years and ten, I find times when it lifted itself out of its impurities of spasms and routines and became, usually briefly, as if shaped by a poet or storyteller. When the time was short and intense, like one of Wordsworth's "Spots of Time," it became, alas for a moment only, a lyric poem. If it went on through time and took in characters and events, it became a story. Now, looking back at my life, I see it largely as a sheaf of unarranged poems and stories with a few threads binding them together. I don't remember much of what happened in between. What I remember most about my life is its literature.

I don't want at my age to go metaphysical, but I doubt that there are, outside us in X, assortments of ready-made poems and stories and that we just happen along and find roles in them. It takes a poet and a storyteller to make a poem and a story. Even if such literary works are lying ready-made outside us in X, it takes a poet and a storyteller to recognize them when they come along.

As perhaps several of you know, I turned to writing stories of my own life to fill a gap left by my retirement and the death of my wife. I had the good fortune of having been brought up in the early part of this century in the woods of western Montana and of not having to go to school until I was nearly eleven. My collection of stories is called *A River Runs Through It*, and they are love stories: stories of my love of craft—of what men and women can do with their hands—and of my love of seeing life turn into literature.

The reaction to these stories suggests that at times I may have succeeded. One of the stories, entitled "USFS 1919," is about my third summer in the early United States Forest Service, when I was seventeen years old, but older than the Forest Service. It is, if anything, overloaded with the excitement of learning how to do things in the woods of northern Idaho and how it feels to do them, of how, for instance, to fight forest fires and how it feels when the heat is so great that the only oxygen left is less than fourteen inches from the ground. But now in my hometown of Missoula, Montana, I am something of a hero to the big-legged boys and girls who are back-packers—they stop to congratulate me because an excerpt from this story was published in the *Backpacking Journal*. The excerpt contains a brief sketch of the history of the art of packing horses, mules, and camels—of its origins in Asia, its travels across Africa and from there by way of the Arabs to Spain, where it picked up much of its present terminology (such as *manty* and the *cinch* of a saddle), and from Spain to Mexico and from Mexico to squaws and from squaws to us. To the big-legged boys and girls of my hometown, no greater honor can befall a living writer than to have something published in the *Backpacking Journal*, especially if it tells how to throw a diamond hitch.

But I have had several letters about this story from some girls from Brooklyn that pleased me even more. The overall plot of my Forest Service story is that of a boy in the woods who for the first time sees his life turning into a story, and the girls from Brooklyn, where supposedly one tree grows, wrote to tell me that they liked my story of the boy in the Forest Service in northern Idaho in 1919 because that very summer (1976) the same thing had happened to them—for the first time ever they had seen their own lives turn into a story. I don't know what had happened to them—perhaps they had fallen in love with some boy in a summer camp in upstate New York—but what was even more important to them is that for the first time they had seen their lives have a complication and a purgation.

No doubt, much of their power to make such an observation is genetic, but I am sure some of it can be taught. If I did not think so, I would not have spent fifty years of my life trying to teach literature, in good times and in bad times.

The Woods,
Books, and
Truant Officers

Norman Maclean*

*   *   *

Just how much I learned from my afternoon schooling in the woods, you are to judge, especially if you are experts at what I am talking about. I dedicated *A River Runs Through It and Other Stories* to my children and also to experts. I meant these stories in part to be a record of how certain things were done just before the world of most of history ended—most of history being a world of hand and horse and hand tools and horse tools. I meant to record not only how we did certain things well in that world now almost beyond recall, but how it felt to do those things well that are now slipping from our hands and memory. I meant when I said we fished with an eight-and-a-half-foot rod weighing four and a half ounces that it was a rod and not a pole and that it was four and a half ounces and not four, and if it had been four ounces it would have been an eight-and not an eight-and-a-half-foot rod; and I also

*"The Woods, Books, and Truant Officers" by Norman Maclean is reprinted from *Chicago*. Copyright © 1977 by Norman Maclean. Reprinted with the permission of the publisher.

meant that when the rod trembled in our hands our hearts trembled with it.

But it is the morning part of my schooling that should be of most concern to us collectively, for it was in the morning that my father helped with the writing part of this book. The morning was divided into three hourly periods. We started at nine and ended at noon, and each of the three hours was divided into two parts, one of 45 minutes when I studied in my room across the hall from his, and 15 minutes when I recited to him in his study. I cannot tell you how much of life 15 minutes can be when you are six, seven, eight, nine, or ten years old and alone with a red-headed Presbyterian minister and cannot answer one of his questions and he won't go on to the next and there is no one else in the room he can turn to and ask and it is going to be the same way tomorrow.

But I can tell you that none of these three hourly periods was devoted to show-and-tell or to the development of personality, mine or his. They were devoted exclusively to reading and writing; while the kids my age in school were learning their ABC's, he was trying to teach me how to write the American language. John Stuart Mill boasts that his father taught him to read Greek when he was so young that English almost became his second language. I have been a little slower to develop, being 73 before I thought I could write the American language as my father tried to teach it to me.

Three basic things he pounded into me long ago about this book that I started to write after reaching my Biblical allotment of three score years and ten.

(1) Being a Scot, he tried to make me write economically. He tried to make me write primarily with nouns and verbs, and not to fool around with adjectives and adverbs, not even when I wanted to write soul stuff. At nine o'clock, when the first period began, he would assign me a 200-word theme; at the end of the ten o'clock period he would tell me, "Now rewrite it in 100 words"; and he concluded the morning by telling me, "Now, throw it away." Sometimes in my study room alone I shed as many tears as I sacrificed words. In the next period, to brace me up, he would say, "My boy, never be too proud to save a single word."

(2) To perceive clearly another characteristic of the writing in this book, you will have to realize that both my father and my mother were first-generation immigrants. Indeed I am told that when my father came to this country he had a heavy Scottish burr, but it had disappeared by the time I first remember him. Great as his pride was in his Scottish background, it had to make way for his love of his new land, and, as a small sign of his love, he tried to remove his burr and speak American. He despised Presbyterian ministers who came from Scotland and floated from church to church in this country trying to pick up a living by keeping on the move. My father swore that they were all fourth-raters in Scotland, where they couldn't make a living, and that they made a pitiful living in America only by exaggerating their Scottish burrs so their congregations would think they were the original Church of Scotland. By the time I can remember my father, he had no burr, but his speech, although flawless, was more English than American—and he knew it. So, like many other first-generation immigrants, he put upon the shoulders of his first-born son the job of becoming completely an American. I was taught to listen and then listen some more to American speech—its idioms and turns of phrase, its grammatical structures, and its rhythms. Then, I was told that I should take these pieces of American speech and put them together into something at least fresh and interesting and at times into something strange and beautiful if I could. You can start looking for this characteristic of style with the opening sentences of my stories: "I was young, and I thought I was tough, and I knew it was beautiful, and I was a little bit crazy but hadn't noticed it yet." "I was young" . . . "thought I was tough" . . . "was a little bit crazy" . . . and "hadn't noticed it yet" are all ordinary pieces of American speech, but they allow something to sneak in unnoticed that is not a part of ordinary speech but is key to the whole feeling of the story, "I knew it was beautiful." In addition, these pieces, when put together in their grammatical structures and rhythms, should fit together in no ordinary manner.

One of my editors admitted to me that he spent two evenings looking through the Bible and Biblical concordances for the source of the title of the book, *A River Runs Through It*. But its source, as far as I know, is in such an ordinary farmer's expression as "a creek runs through the north forty," listed to beauty perhaps by the substitution of "river" for "creek" and "it" for "the north forty." The liquid R's that begin and end "river" are to be contrasted to the grunting K's that begin and end "creek"; and the farmer's "north forty" (forty acres being a 16th of a square mile or section of land) is to be contrasted to the substituted "it" which is the "it" of the world to come and the "it" of Shakespeare, as in, "If it be now, 'tis not to come." Also, the farmer's ordinary phrase is without rhythm, made up, except for "forty," of staccato one-syllable words, whereas the two syllables of "river" turn "A river runs" into running rhythm, the rhythm running over three alliterative R's. So my father is also co-author of the title of this book, *A River Runs Through It*.

(3) My final acknowledgement is that it was my father from whom I first learned rhythm, perhaps without his or my quite knowing it. Every morning we had what was called "family worship." After breakfast and again after what was called supper, my father read to us from the Bible or from some religious poet such as Wordsworth; then we knelt by our chairs while my father prayed. My father read beautifully. He avoided the homiletic sing-song most ministers fall into when they look inside the Bible or edge up to poetry, but my father overread poetry a little so that none of us, including him, could miss the music.

Although since retirement I seem to have turned to the narrative art, most of the courses I have taught have been in poetry, and unlike teachers of poetry who devote most of their courses to the psyche and society, I always devoted a big portion of each course in poetry to rhythm—quantitative and qualitative, accentual and intonational and superimposed rhythms.

Twice a day when I was very young I heard my father read such English as: "The Lord is my shepherd; I shall not want. He maketh me to lie down in green pastures; he leadeth me beside the still waters. He restoreth my soul; he leadeth me in the paths of righteousness for his name's sake. Yea, though I walk through the valley of the shadow of death, I will fear no evil; for thou art with me; thy rod and thy staff they comfort me.''

And so to the end of the 23rd Psalm, by the way with only two adjectives, *green* pastures and *still* waters, both of them immortal, which is the right way to use adjectives if you can't stay away from them. As for rhythm, it may be said that I learned rhythm early on bended knees.

Of course, when I was between six and ten and a half I didn't know anything about superimposed rhythms; I only knew when I heard my father read the 23rd Psalm that I could hear the still waters moving and pausing and the Lord comforting me. Now, since I have long been a teacher, I can say that it is a wonderful example of superimposed rhythms, although I always try to remember in making an analytical statement like that to remember the still waters and the Lord's comfort. Still, I can count at least three concurrent rhythms in the harp of David. There is, perhaps most obviously, what we can call quantitative rhythm, a patterned recurrence of speech groups of almost the same length or quantity. Concurrent with this quantitative rhythm is a second rhythm; in each quantitative unit there is a repetition of or a coming close to the same grammatical structure, which we shall call a grammatical rhythm—the repetition of subject, verb, and predicate in that order. Let us listen to just these two at first, the patterned recurrence of length and grammatical structure: "The Lord is my shepherd; I shall not want. He maketh me to lie down in green pastures; he leadeth me beside the still waters." But listen now to the lovely variants of patterns so that the song is a song and not a sing-song of mechanical repetition. In "thy rod and thy staff they comfort me," the subject still comes first but instead of being just one word as "I" or "He" or two words as "The Lord," it is now six words. "Thy rod and thy staff, they," and so the verb is only one word and the predicate only one, "comfort me." And what about other such lovely variants, as "Yea, though I walk through the valley of the shadow"?

These two rhythms, what we have called quantitative and grammatical rhythms, are deep in Hebrew poetry, but present also in the King James translation is the modern base rhythm of English poetry—accentual rhythm, or, as we used to say in school, "the stuff that scans," where what recurs is what we called "feet" when I was young, although I believe now in high school and even college feet go nameless and perhaps unnoticed. The foot is a unit of two or more syllables that are disproportionately stressed, and, when the first syllable is relatively unstressed and the second stressed it is called an iamb and when the first two syllables are relatively unstressed and the last one stressed it is called an anapest. Furthermore, when the rhythmical pattern is a patterned recurrence of either or both of these feet, we shall call it here falling-rising rhythm, and we shall not bother about the opposite, rising-falling, made up of trochees and dactyls, because the King James version of the 23rd Psalm is in falling-rising rhythm, made up of iambs and anapests, which are often changing place for variety and richness, both being falling-rising rhythms and easily interchanged. The first line of the psalm opens and closes with an iamb and two anapests in between:

> Thĕ Lórd / iš m̃y shép / hĕrd: Ĭ sháll/
> nŏt wánt.

The psalm ends with a line that likewise has two anapests in the middle and an iamb at the end (with a feminine ending) but opens with two iambs instead of one:

> Ănd Í / wĭll dwéll / ĭn thĕ hóuse /
> ŏf thĕ Lórd / fŏrévĕr.

There are, then, at least three kinds of rhythms going on at the same time in this translation of David's psalm—quantitative, grammatical, and accentual—and three rhythms all at once are a lot of rhythm for a little poem that is marked as being six lines long, and especially since there is always the danger of poetry becoming too poetical. Important for us, too, there is always the danger of prose seeming to be poetical at all. It is perhaps enough to say here that the 23rd Psalm does not bang out its rhythms, but hovers about them, sometimes stating them precisely so the ear knows what it is listening for, then drifting off into the dim shadows of rhythms, and then bouncing back into sunshine rhythm again.

The questions raised by rhythm in prose are too big to go into here, so I will not start any arguments but instead just state a few of what to me are axioms about rhythm and prose. You don't have to believe them but you can bet they're true. (1) All prose should be rhythmical. (2) One should practically never be consciously aware of the rhythms of prose; one should be aware only that it is a pleasure to read what one is reading. (3) There are, of course, exceptions to my statement that prose rhythms should not be noticeable— there are times indeed when rhythms should be both seen and heard, as for instance, when one is fooling around and showing off. I will quote again the opening sentence of the story "USFS 1919," which I used earlier as a sentence made out of American idioms, but it comes back now as an example of a sentence having the three kinds of rhythms of the 23rd Psalm—quantitative, grammatical, and accentual. "I was young, and I thought I was tough, and I knew it was beautiful, and I was a little bit crazy but hadn't noticed it yet." It is a showoff sentence, and the rhythms go with it, but I couldn't go around writing many sentences like that in a row without getting challenged. (4) The fourth and final axiom is that there are places in prose where the reader not only will accept but expects a great deal of rhythm—where he will notice an absence of rhythm and take it as a deficiency not only in the writing but in the author. If an author writes out of a full heart and rhythms don't come with it then something is missing inside the author. Perhaps a full heart.

*   *   *

Teaching and Story Telling: Talk at University of Chicago and Montana State University

Norman Maclean*

It is interesting to see what you end up doing. With me at least, it has been two things, or at least putting two things together. One thing is what you have done all your professional life, and the other is something you wanted to do when you were young. It would be crazy to give up what you have become expert in doing professionally—it would probably be impossible to, but you have to watch all the time to see that it doesn't take charge so that you go on doing the same thing over and over again, which isn't what you wanted to end up doing. You wanted to end up preserving something that was young in you, but was put aside with other youthful things.

The title indicates my two things. I taught for nearly half a century, but I started to tell stories before I taught. There is a good deal of overlap, though, between teaching and story telling, and was, even in my early life; as for my stories, teaching is almost everywhere present in them. In fact, one of the compliments I keep

*"Teaching and Storytelling" by Norman Maclean is reprinted from the text of the speech Norman Maclean delivered at the University of Chicago on February 19, 1978, and at Montana State University in Bozeman, April 20, 1978. Copyright © 1978 by Norman Maclean.

least secret is a letter from a Ph.D. candidate in biology at the University of Montana who wrote that he regarded the story, "A River Runs Through It," as the finest manual written on the art of fly fishing in the northwest. It's not a secret either that I feel equally flattered because no other critic seems to have noticed that I am teaching nearly all the time in my stories. I take this negative compliment, perhaps incorrectly, as evidence that I have been fairly successful in combining the two parts of my title.

And make no mistake that my stories are loaded with teaching. My second story, "Logging and Pimping, and 'Your Pal, Jim,' " short as it is, is also something of a manual on logging, especially on the art of the sawyer before there were power saws, together with some hesitant suggestions on the art of pimping. As for the last story in the collection, "USFS 1919: The Ranger, the Cook, and a Hole in the Sky," it is almost a syllabus for a history course on the early United States Forest Service before most of history ended, history being all the ages in which men and women did with their hands and feet what horses, mules, and camels couldn't do for them. In fact, I consider myself a historian of the hands and feet of the men and women of my part of the country.

It couldn't be otherwise. I did not start writing stories until after I retired from teaching and, once a teacher always a teacher. When I am fishing and look upstream and see another fisherman coming down the opposite side I wait until I see him cast and then I say to myself, "C minus."

The presence of teaching in all my stories isn't only a matter of being professionally conditioned. For me at least, it is a matter of belief. I put it to you this way. If you hoped to write something beautiful, wouldn't it be all right to hope that, in addition, it would be true in some revealing and interesting ways, and what would be wrong with going on and hoping it would also be good? What would be wrong with hoping to make something beautiful, true, and good? In my heart, arguments about these questions are only attempts to create a field called aesthetics, and I do not have time enough left in life for such monkey-business. So I accept as another negative compliment the fact that no one has challenged any factual statement in my stories—no one from the Bitterroot has written or said to me, "You say it is 28 miles from Elk Summit to the mouth of Blodgett Canyon, but it is 31 miles." Not even a fisherman has challenged anything I have said, and most fisherman are looking more for arguments than for fish.

One more guess as to why there is so much teaching in my stories, and then to some of the artistic problems that arise when teaching becomes an important part of a story, because, as we all know, teaching and story telling can easily destroy each other—a story is dead if it seems to preach and a teacher is also dead if he spins yarns and hasn't anything to say.

The final reason I try to do both at the same time has to do with the way I was brought up. I was brought up in western Montana, and by the time I was fourteen I was working in the woods every summer, either in the United States Forest Service or in logging camps, and I worked every summer in the woods until I started teaching at the University of Chicago in 1928. During the fifty years since, I have returned every summer to a log cabin my father and I built in 1921, on a lake south of Glacier Park, and now that I am retired I spend about a third of each year there sixteen miles from everlasting snow. So, if I am a story teller, I got my early training in a bunkhouse, and, if you are familiar with the bunkhouse variety of the narrative art, you can see readily that my present stories still have these humble origins. When I first went in the woods I was so young I just listened to the masters—but even then things fundamental to the art began to appear. I saw early that oral stories have to be short. No matter who you are, don't expect even your closest friends to listen to one of your stories for ten minutes. Even so, the chances are that before you are half through your wife will interrupt you. So, if I had still another life to live I couldn't conceive of a novel—I would be sure ahead of time that a novel would be mostly wind, as most novels are. Early, too, I learned that your friends won't listen to a story unless a lot happens in it. None of your friends in a bunkhouse is being psychoanalyzed and is willing to spend money year after year waiting for something to happen. In a bunkhouse the governing motto of both psycho-analysis and the narrative art is, "Pick up your bed and walk."

Oddly, though, another characteristic of the western story is that practically always it has something to do with truth, but it was only later that I realized how complicated the relations are. On a simple level, I learned a lot about the outdoor world from bunkhouse stories, for instance, the difference between a sawbuck and a Decker pack saddle and a California and a Texas cowboy saddle, and those are good things to know. I was also taught that the world was funny and full of pain, and that, too, is a good thing to know.

I didn't get a chance to tell stories, though, until I got back to town. There I found a few pals about my age who also wanted to tell stories. Although foolishly the foolish legend continues that story telling is a universal instinct extending back to primitive man who supposedly spent his evenings in caves spinning yarns, the truth is most people are afraid to tell stories, nearly all the rest don't know when to stop, all of which leaves, as I said, only a few good story tellers.

I found only three my age—a French-Canadian, who worked the mill pond for a big saw mill and so followed the French-Canadian tradition of always being on water in the woods; the school's leading piano player, as we called him, who had spent a summer in Paris taking lessons and came back playing Debussy who, we thought, was off-key but the girls didn't; and my brother, who while he lived was a great news reporter. We sat in the moonlight on the wide steps of the First National Bank of Missoula, Montana. A great river runs through the center of our town and the bank is at one end of the bridge. So we sat trying to learn to tell stories in the moonlight beside a great river. And I learned again that stories have to be short with a lot happening in them and I learned again that people like to learn as well as pull the long bow, but unless you know what you are doing, teaching can kill a story. It seems as if what you learn about story telling generally is only a more intense form of what you already knew because I learned again that a story should be funny as well as full of pain. I enlarged this knowledge later when I discovered that hilarity and agony are both necessary to salvation.

We told stories many nights but only until 9 o' clock. Perhaps the other three had made a secret agreement, or perhaps their baser instincts worked on the same time-clock, but at 9 they all faded into moonlight each chasing some girl. What was to be expected from a French-Canadian, a reporter, a piano player who had taken summer lessons in Paris? (Each had a chick, and the piano player who had taken summer lessons in Paris found nothing discordant in having several.)

But I always had still another story and wanted someone who wanted to listen to it, someone who never came along after 9 o'clock in Missoula, Montana. It was so long ago that garbage cans had just been installed at street corners, and so long ago that they were not yet chained to lamp posts. I was frustrated with unexpressed and possibly inexpressible creativity, which eventually I transferred to the garbage cans, so I began to carry them to the middle of the bridge and flip them over the side. It was such a long way down to the river that you had to tell by sound whether they hit on their sides, which was without art, or whether they instantly sank, bottom up, a dead hit. You could tell by the sound, just as you can tell whether you have hit a deer just back of the shoulder blade where the heart is. There is definitely such a thing as a dead sound and it sounds just exactly as if you had sunk a garbage can. I was getting expert in giving the can just the right flip so it would hit the river with the mouth open and gasp, when a policeman appeared out of this same moonlight previously spoken of as poetic. I could see him the length of the bridge and I waited until he got close enough to lean on the rail and watch the next flip, and sure enough, it didn't flip right and landed on its side and floated at least a quarter of a mile in plain view in the moonlight before it sank. The policeman had a daughter and he knew I thought she was beautiful, so leaning on the rail and watching the garbage can float in the moonlight, he told me to come back next day in bathing trunks and fish out the garbage cans and then come back late the same night when no one could see me and put the garbage cans back on the street corners. Which, by the way, is a kind of a poor ending for a story told by someone who was trying to learn how to be a story teller, except for some reason it has become a part of me and I can tell by the sound every time I finish a paragraph whether it lit on its side or was shot behind the shoulder where the heart is.

The sum of all this, I suppose, is that fairly early in life I learned beside a river in moonlight that story tellers chase chicks—all except me. As for me, I live in a fantasy world playing games with garbage cans, although in the morning they have to be fished out of the creek.

Later in life I enlarged this observation by noting that the world in which you learn to tell stories becomes pretty much the world that gets into your stories—the world in my stories is pretty much a world of moonlight and garbage cans and French-Canadians working on mill ponds, and my brother, and unhappy endings, and, of course a big river running through all of it. I call this the real world, and a lot happens in it.

* * *

So much for background material, as a teacher would say. From here on I would like to concentrate on some of the problems that arise in retirement when trying to put these two parts of my youth together—some large problems and also some dealing with specific pieces of writing, most of them drawn from the story of mine you know best, if you know any of them, the title story, "A River Runs Through It." And first let's try some major problems, although sometimes they are easier to resolve than this or that paragraph— or this sentence even.

The major obligation of a story is *always* to be a story. This is true even if it is the most personal story one will ever tell, as this one is my most personal story. This one is the story of my brother who was murdered. It was my brother who was a master of the art of fly fishing, perhaps the finest in the northwest. It is a story of his father and brother who were expert fishermen—not as good as he was but perhaps necessarily more expert because they did not have his genius. Our chief claim to be in the story is that we loved to watch him fish. It is a story of my brother who had another side to him—at least we heard he had, and maybe most of the time we believed he had but we were never sure, and were never to be sure. We knew, though, he was a gambler and had a packstring of women and we heard he was behind in the big stud poker game at Hot Springs and beyond a doubt in Montana it is not good to be behind in a stud game at a hot springs. In our Scottish family, the family and religion were the center of the universe, and, like Scots, we did not believe we should praise each other but should always love and be ready to help each other, only we never seemed able to help my brother, being hesitant because we were not often sure he needed help—in fact, were not sure we understood him, and we were also hesitant because we looked clumsy when we tried to be of help, and he looked like what he was, an artist whose Scottish pride was offended by a clumsy offer of help. So, in the end when he was murdered, we did not know whether it had been just a case of his being stuck up in an alley and beaten to death or whether he was paying some debt he owed in his other life.

In the end all we knew—really knew—about him was that he was beautiful and dead and we had not helped. And, through him all we came to know about mankind my father summed up when he said: "It is those we live with and love and should know who elude us."

Something like this, crudely stated, is the story. Anything that goes into the story from reality or the imagination must be with it and for it. As an instance, there are a fair number of descriptions in this story of streams and mountains, nature descriptions I think they are called, but none should have been admitted unless they are contributions to the story. They should bring out my brother's beauty or our love. In our family, men folk did not go around saying they loved each other. In our family, nature was a medium of our love, a carrier of it, an object of it, a cause of it. We loved each other because we loved the same sights and sounds and rivers, because we recognized, not only that we were parts of it but that all of us in some ways were masters of it—swinging an axe, building our log cabins, leading ducks on the wing, noting Caddis flies hatching from the bottom of shallow water in early September, and just leaning on the oars at sunset. And we knew that nature was often the master of us, and we loved both nature and ourselves because of that. Any description of nature in this story has something to do about family love.

The answer, then, as how either descriptions or teaching or anything else can find their ways into a story is simple to state but harder to realize. They have to be parts of the story, and the test of whether they are is also simple to state—a so-called teaching part cannot be pulled out of a story without leaving a gap in the story.

Another large question to be answered is how much of what subjects can be made parts of a story. Let's start on this by recalling my pleasure because a Ph.D. in biology at the University of Montana wrote that my first story was a manual on the art of fly fishing. I had hoped it would be and for it to be a manual of an art, that is, a poetics of an art, all the main elements of the art of fly fishing would have to be presented together with insights into what constitutes excellence in each element. So in this story there are detailed instructions on how to cast, how to read water—that is, how to tell where the fish are biting—how to fish different kinds of water, how to hook fish, and how to play and land them—the works, so to speak. But the second story in the collection does not try to present the whole art of logging—it pictures only the art of being a sawyer and says nothing whatsoever, for instance, about the art of timber cruising or scaling logs.

The large answer to large questions is getting to be the same, as it should be if you have something in mind when you write. The answer to the question of what and how much teaching should be in a story is what and how much does the story call for. The logging story is about two rival sawyers who try to outsaw each other, and that's the answer—the reader has to know enough about the art of sawing to know what it would be like to be killed off at one end of a saw. As for the manual on fly fishing, it is essential to the story that you believe my brother was a master of the art and to be a master of the art is to be on top of the art. But it is not enough for this story that you know and can judge the art—you must know what it feels like to perform the art and what it looks like when it is performed by an artist. In other words, when the story is through it should be not only a poetics of the art but the poetry of the art.

It is essential that the story be both the poetics and poetry of fly fishing because, unless you can see and feel about my brother as his father and brother did, I have no story to tell about him.

The order in which the parts of a poetics should be presented also raises many questions, only a few of which will be touched on here. My working-day is usually divided in two—in the mornings I write and later in the day, perhaps in the late afternoon but certainly some time before going to bed, I take a bath and stay in it until the water goes cold thinking about what I am going to write the next morning. It is hard enough to write without at the same time having to start thinking about what to write. I like to have the main problems of order settled, the episode that is coming next, and the manner in which it is to be presented, that is, through whose eyes it is to be seen so I will know ahead of time what I may permit myself to see and feel and what not. All this is wordless, it is architectural, and you cannot make a mistake or the structure cracks or may even collapse. Although it is that important a part of story telling, I refer to it, possibly so I won't be afraid of it, ''as the bathtub part of writing.''

A lot of water turned cold before I could make myself start the story with casting. Casting is highly technical and difficult. It's hard enough to teach someone to cast when he is standing right next to you on a dock holding your rod and you're holding his wrist. It would be easy to scare off most readers at the start by trying to tell them how to cast an 8½ foot, 4½ ounce rod on a four-count rhythm between 2 and 10 o'clock (12 o'clock being straight overhead), but that was the way it had to be—not much can be taught about fly fishing to someone unless he knows how to start with something about casting since everything else depends upon his being able to get his flies out where the fish are. So it was primarily for teaching reasons that four of the first five pages of my story are devoted to the art of casting, and I could have written this essay about the pain they cost. On the other hand, it seemed almost inevitable dramatically to end with my brother's landing a big fish, but often, what seems inevitable structurally comes with artistic pain, even if the pain is not allowed to show. For instance, there have to be tricks in your wrist artistically to catch fish all through a long story and never land one until page 99.

I promised to say something at the end of this story about the end of it and then analyze a few pages from it. Actually, it is not the end of the story but the last time my brother is seen in the story— after this, we only hear. What we know both of teaching and of story telling makes it almost inevitable that he should last be seen landing a big fish and that for the first time we should see something of what is involved in landing a big one. But what we know about both arts tells us that this is not nearly enough to see of him at the end. We should see him for the first and last time as a master of *all* parts of the art of fly fishing—casting, reading the water, selecting flies, hooking a fish—and then, by God, landing him. A teacher would say at the end there should be a summary of the subject. But a story teller and perhaps also a teacher would say even this is not enough—the end is a climax as well as a summary, so at the end he should do something spectacular and it should require the highest gifts of all and the highest gifts are mental. So in this penultimate scene he does something requiring great perception and deduction but deduction from great knowledge of the life of amphibian insects, of the underwater, invisible parts of nature. It is a rather remarkable piece of detective work in reading the water and in selecting the right fly, and, believe me, these are mental achievements.

The details of this portion of the penultimate scene when my brother becomes a Sherlock Holmes of the art will have to be supplied by your recollection or future discovery because there is just time enough left to watch him from a distance land his last fish.

And before we turn to this part, there is just time enough to point out two or three things about it, and no more lest we overwhelm the story with story telling. One thing surely, the penultimate scene should convey the sense of the finality not only of an art but of him, for, in a page he will be dead. So it is at a distance that he is seen landing his last fish, he and his art fading already into an abstraction of art and of himself. He and his rod become a water figure and a wand. But as he fades out of reality great technical problems arise— for instance, the problems of intelligibility. Most of your readers won't know anything about fly fishing and to them the movements of a fly fisherman even up close don't make sense. The problem of course is much more complicated by the fact that you are really not writing for novices—you hope your most devoted readers will be experts, and you have had this hope all the time, so all the time you have had a dual audience of opposites, one to whom you have little to teach and the other to whom you have to teach everything. It's something like teaching an extension course, but in any event you are up against what teachers of narration call the problem of show and tell, and you had better not be simple-minded, as many moderns are, who believe everything should be shown. If you do, what you will show will seem unintelligible to most readers. The artistic job to be done for the novice is to transform absurdity into knowledge and artistry; for the expert, it is to make him feel that what he knows and can do well is beautiful.

Let's mention but not proceed with a simultaneous problem. It should be mentioned but without involvement here. How at a great distance do you represent the power and motions of my brother's *underwater* rival, the big fish?

As a minimum, certainly, the eyes of another artist are needed, an artist not so good as the one shown landing the fish but good enough to tell you the meaning and beauty of the motions of the water figure and his wand, which are all that are shown. Actually, there are two inferior artists present to transform into artistry what would otherwise seem to many as erratic and mysterious motions; as it is, the water figure is seen as seen by his father and brother, who love him and will forever grieve for him, two facts to become necessary parts of this story, which, despite all the talk so far about fishing, is not really a fishing story.

* * *

[The episode referred to here is reprinted on pp. 32–37 in this volume.]

A Man I Met
in Mann Gulch

Norman Maclean*

I'm puzzled as to why I am to talk to you on this or any other occasion, and you certainly must be. There can be only one possible general explanation—most of us, at least many of us, must live two lives. Neither one ever fully, because whichever life we live more completely leaves us with a sense of incompleteness, but one life we live more ostensibly than the other, so that in *Who's Who* we are put down as a university professor or a forester—never both, although oddly many of us are or have been both. There is no other half-convincing explanation to account for my presence here tonight than that after I retired from the English Department at the University of Chicago five years beyond retirement age I decided to spend my declining years—my doctor always corrects me consolingly and says I should say my remaining years—in blowing upon the embers of my first life, which I left smoldering behind me one half a century ago here in the woods of western Montana.

Because until the month in 1928 when I started teaching English

*"A Man I Met in Mann Gulch: Talk at the Intermountain Fire Research Council" by Norman Maclean is reprinted from the text of the speech Norman Maclean delivered in Missoula, Montana on October 31, 1979. Copyright © 1979 by Norman Maclean.

at the University of Chicago I had planned—almost carefully planned—to be a logger. I planned it carefully according to my size. When I was 14 and not big enough to handle boards all day, I started working in the box factory of Polley's saw mill here in Missoula just across the Bitterroot tracks; as I got to the size of boards I was shifted to the assorting table, where all you do is pull boards as they come out of the mill and put them in piles. It is by ways like this that you know you are growing older in the saw mills—this and by counting the number of fingers you have had sawed off. When I shifted from the saw mills to the woods I started with their beauty—I had been in the Boy Scout troop of K. D. Swan, the fine photographer of the early Forest Service who in a perhaps lesser way did for the Forest Service what the great photographer William H. Jackson did for Yellowstone Park before it was a park, and K. D. hired me as his assistant on one of his photographic expeditions into the far away wilderness of what was then the Selway National Forest. From him I learned early to look at mountains stylistically— as designs and compositions needing only my appearance as a beholder for them to become objects of art.

The next step was a shock, forever leaving all childish things behind me and forever, so I thought for a while, making a man of me. For the next two summers I worked for one of the toughest and most legendary old-time rangers in the Forest Service in the Elk Summit District which itself is a legend and already was one then.

These were the days when the toughest guy in town was hired as the Forest Service Ranger. Bill Bell was the toughest in the whole Bitterroot Valley, and so was his dog, which was half grey hound and half bull dog, and made him the fastest and fiercest. In late autumn word would come to Missoula that Bill was in a big fight up at Lolo Hot Springs with some trapper who was trying to take over his trap line. At first we were afraid we had missed something, but we soon learned that we still had plenty of time to make it over the forty bad miles of road to the Hot Springs and see Bill finish the fight—often with one of the Olson brothers who, when Bill wasn't around, would fight each other for several days at a time just to get in shape for Bill.

It was from Bill that I learned about fire-fighting and perhaps even more about life. Being still a kid I was started off as a lookout. There was nothing on top of the mountain where he showed me how to be a lookout but him and me, a map board, an alidade, and a scattering of dead trees all struck by lightning. After he showed me how to orient a map and locate a fire, he added, "That pack hanging on the pole of the tent in the basin is because you're also smoke chaser up here. Any time, night or day, you spot a fire in your district you put your pack on your back and start for the fire." When I finally recovered my voice in the thin altitude, I asked, "What do you do then?" He looked away at a low cloud that might have been smoke (as far as I knew), and answered, "Put it out." I was just getting to my big question, "What if I can't?" He looked astonished that there was an answer to the question. "Run for help," he said. The only time I or anyone else ever called him Mr. Bell was when I asked, "Mr. Bell, how long do you stay on a fire before you run for help?" He then made an answer I have used many times since and in many situations in life. He said, "Before you run for help, stay on a fire twice as long as you think you can't handle it alone."

It's odd how many crises will cool off in life if you can only stand a double-dose of heat.

Probably the most exact reason I returned to Missoula for this occasion was to give you the once-over so I could get some idea of what I might have looked like if I had continued to follow my first life and was a part of the audience tonight. To tell you the truth, you look a lot better than I thought you would. In my day there was nothing between a forest fire and a fire fighter but a Pulaski, often a real old time Pulaski, that originally had been a double-bitted axe and now had one bit cut off and a little hoe welded on where the bit had been. Behind the fire fighter there was nothing but a strawboss who kept saying, "Keep your damn head down." I used to wonder what a second- or third-generation fire fighter would look like, if there was anything to the theory of the inheritance of acquired characteristics. I used to draw pictures of second- and third-generation fire fighters resembling potato pickers, with noses in the ground, asses pointing to the solar system, backbones with the vertebrae fused together into a bow, kidneys totally disappeared from disuse, little short legs and a grunt. I even designed a plaster-of-paris right-angle corset fitting those specifications for fire fighters to lace themselves into when they went on shift. It would remove any hope at the outset of ever being classified as erectus.

So I am pleasantly surprised to see all of you are sufficiently advanced in the evolutionary scheme of things to be standing or sitting. It removes some of the fear I had that I might relapse biologically when I retired from teaching. The truth is that you look quite a bit like a bunch of university professors, and my guess is that most of you are. There must be a lot of overlap between the two professions, and my guess also is that I wouldn't have looked much different from what I do now if I had spent my life backfiring, as I did anyway. I don't know how you avoid backfiring in life—chemical deterrents don't seem to help much whenever the gulches get narrow.

The set of motives that brought me here tonight must be much the same as the motives that upon my retirement from teaching at 70 turned me to writing stories about the woods when I was young. The first collection of my stories, *A River Runs Through It*, is heavily autobiographical, but the long story I am working on now is the tragic story of the Mann Gulch fire in which 13 out of 16 smokejumpers were burned to death within 56 minutes after they had collected and folded their parachutes. It is true I was on the fire before it was completely contained but it certainly is not an autobiographical story, at least not in the usual sense, and many of the motives attracting me to it will be forever unknown to me. Though I search for them from time to time, I promise I will not go in for self-analysis tonight. Who knows what the power of fire is over us? Over us as individuals and over the human race from its beginning? The power of fire is so multiform that it often seems contradictory, and so the fires of hell are the symbol of humanity's passion, hate and eternal damnation, and the ''eternal flame'' is the symbol of our hope for eternal peace and salvation. No doubt many of fire's eternal powers have brought us here together at this same table tonight. No doubt all of us could say with Robert Frost, "Some say the world will end in fire,/Some say in ice./From what I've suffered of desire/I hold with those who favor fire. . . ." But a banquet talk should stop far short of poetry, and even shorter of psychoanalysis. For after-dinner let's try something much simpler than the power of fire.

I am drawn here tonight not only by fire's hidden powers but much more openly by the fact that I have always liked fire fighters and have always wanted to be one. The fact that I am also something of a story teller only enhances my feelings for both forest fires and fire fighters—fires make good stories and fire fighters are usually good story tellers. Before I sit down tonight I'd like to tell you simply about three or four fire fighters I have come to know through my study of the Mann Gulch fire who have helped make me feel that in my retirement I have enlarged my appreciation of life and extended the boundaries of my compassion and pleasure. I repeat, I have come to know them through returning to the Mann Gulch fire, but I must add that I have never met any of them. I have come to know them as a story teller comes to know people without having to meet them. Many of you know them both ways—as story tellers and as friends of theirs. But one thing I know as the result of having taught for exactly half a century. I know I can't talk carefully about three or four people in the time I have left to talk, especially to an audience who knows what I am talking about better than I do. Before this audience I will do well to bring one fire fighter back alive and hopefully freshen his image a little, and, if I have time to talk about only one, then there is one above all others who draws you and me and Mann Gulch together.

In a Symposium entitled without a blush of modesty, "Fire Control for the 80's," a small space must be found open in which to speak of the legendary first scientist of your science, the study of fire behavior. In an early work entitled *Fire Behavior*, printed in 1951, Jack Barrows says that, although "forestry dates back hundreds of years, organized research has been underway only about 30 years." Anybody can subtract "about 30 years" from 1951 and come up with 1921, 1922 or 1923, and anybody who knows anything about

Jack Barrows knows he was one of Harry T. Gisborne's early and favorite prodigies in the science of fire behavior and, if you know Mike Hardy's fine study of *The Gisborne Era*, as you should, you know that on April 1, 1922 Harry Gisborne was made Director of the Priest River Experiment at a salary of $1920.00 per annum. By now you yourself shouldn't have to have been a favorite student of Harry Gisborne to guess that Barrows dates the beginning of the scientific study of fire behavior with Gisborne's appointment in 1922 as Director of the Priest River Experiment. As a student of the Mann Gulch fire, I came to know him at the extreme opposite end of his career—on the day of his death, and, as a result, the title of this talk when published will be, "A Man I Met in Mann Gulch." Today is ten days less than 30 years since Gisborne's death there, and yet I, a much later student, still like 1922 as the beginning of the scientific study of fire behavior, provided of course that in a large context one understands no science has had a beginning since man began. We have always wondered.

On November 9 of the year of the fire, 1949, Harry Gisborne left Helena in a Jeep with one of his favorite young rangers, Bob Jansson, whom many of you must have known even when he was in school. At the time of the fire, Jansson was Ranger of the Canyon Ferry District, which included Mann Gulch and as Ranger there he had rustled a crew of drunks in the bars of Helena and had brought them down the Missouri to attack the fire in the canyon just upstream from Mann Gulch. While they were trying to jump off the cliffs when shadows of the fire flashed and frightened them, Jansson went down to the mouth of Mann Gulch to get a look-see at the main fire and also to try to establish connections with the smoke-jumpers who he knew had been dropped into Mann Gulch. After the tragedy he had led the rescue crew back into Mann Gulch and remained there until all the black remains were identified by Catholic medallions, snake bite kits, or watches with their hands melted forever at 4 minutes to 6:00. There was good reason, then, for his being selected to be the one to accompany Gisborne on his late autumn quest to find the causes of the Mann Gulch tragedy.

Fortunately for us, he wrote very accurate and vivid prose and fortunately for others besides Gisborne's family, he was asked to write, for purposes of collecting insurance, an accurate and detailed account of the day of Gisborne's death. It must be the best insurance report ever written and certainly one of the classics in the uncollected prose works of the Forest Service. Jansson is one of those I should like to have talked more about if I had time. In some ways he was as much a tragic victim of the fire as any of those whose crosses are on the hillside, although he lived afterwards. The Mann Gulch fire finished him. His nightmares frightened even his dog, who like him would cry all night in the dark; by the following year he was to be transferred to Idaho, and not long after that his family's fatal genetic disease made its first appearance in him. Although he was very demanding of his men and himself, I should like to have worked for him, and I should like to have had more time to work tonight in behalf of his memory.

But we are with him indirectly as he accompanied Harry Gisborne into Mann Gulch on November 9, 1949, and we have glimpses of Gisborne at the dramatic end of his career through the eyes of his devout and worried student.

It is hard to believe that there was much about Harry Gisborne's life and character that did not reveal itself in Mann Gulch on the day of his death, and my guess is that most of us would hope, probably vainly, that we could be almost as completely alive in death as he was. First of all, Gisborne should not have been in Mann Gulch, then or ever again. He had long been a chronic heart patient, but only the strictest orders had stopped him from climbing his 150 foot dead spruce at Priest River to make observations on the different actions of the wind at different elevations. When he received medical orders never to climb his tree again, he said, "What are you telling me? To quit?" If you entertain hope of becoming a legend, as a bare minimum you must be super-dedicated, and if you hope to become a legend as a scientist, you have to be super-dedicated about theories. Gisborne had two theories about the Mann Gulch fire, and he was afraid the coming winter would destroy much of the evidence necessary to test them. No advice could stop him from going into Mann Gulch, which Arthur

D. Moir, then Supervisor of the Helena National Forest, described as "one of the roughest pieces of country east of the Continental Divide."

This pioneer scientist placed above his beloved theories only his beloved facts. Sometimes he referred to facts as "the dope that counts," and I suppose that off-hand we think of him as the master of observing and collating masses of facts, his most lasting monument to this capacity being the first fire danger rating system used successfully on actual fires. There is no doubt that he was the hard-nosed son of a Vermont saw mill operator, and to him theories should result practically in more board feet. When Gisborne entered Mann Gulch, the prevailing theory, advanced by the Forest Service's Board of Review, was that the crew got caught in a pincer movement of two fires—one burning upgulch behind them on their side of the gulch and the other fire burning up the opposite side of the gulch, then circling the head of the gulch and then moving down the crew side of the gulch until it met the crew with the other fire behind it. Jansson quotes Gisborne as taking a good look at the head of the gulch and uttering one sentence, "Not possible for pincer movement to occur because of topography." I'll say not, if for no other reason than that near the head of the gulch there is an exposed reef of rock between a quarter and a half mile in width running from the top of the ridge to the bottom of the gulch that the fire would have had to jump before, equally preposterous, it could then burn around the head of the gulch and run down the other side of it into the teeth of the wind that was blowing the other fire upgulch behind the crew faster than it could move. Odder still, I think there is a good chance that the Board of Review may even have got this literally half-baked theory from Gisborne himself, but whoever conceived it, Gisborne took one look at the lay of the land and gave it up.

Like many pioneer scientists, and I have known a few atomic ones, he mixed hard-boiled facts with a fair number of nutty ideas. They were nutty in a nice kind of way—fanciful, imaginative and even poetical. The most Romantic of Romantic poets, Percy Bysshe Shelley, mixed the most fanciful of visions with what was the most advanced science of his day—even his poems "The Cloud" and "The Ode to the West Wind" are such mixtures of the poetic and scientific imaginations.

On the day Gisborne died he happily saw another of his poetical theories disappear in smoke. He had developed the theory that all fire whirls move in a clockwise motion. Hence, he conjectured that the Mann Gulch fire and other fires resulting from blowouts caused by fire whirls had similar topographical patterns. (1) Ahead of the advancing line of the fire and to the left of it had to be a high promontory. (2) The wind had to be blowing into the fire and so would first shear off the high promontory in front of it and then shear off the advancing fire on its left side. This action of the wind would give a clockwise motion to the fire and so throw spot fires outside it and behind it—evidently if the wind hit the fire on the other side it would give it a counter-clockwise motion and so presumably would drive the fire into itself and there would be no spot fire.

Well, the hard-topographical facts of Mann Gulch don't fit this theory either, and fire whirls can whirl clockwise or counter-clockwise. So Harry Gisborne's last day in Mann Gulch does not give an ample sampling of his lifetime of scientific achievements. But impressive as these are when added up, they are probably not an accurate measurement of his scientific work, a fact probably true of many of the founders of sciences whose actual scientific productions are transcended by some magnetic and intense drawing power of the human spirit. Gisborne was the hard-nosed son of a logger and he was fanciful and daring and poetical, and he must also have been a good teacher, not only partly Shelley but partly Socrates, and, like them, very exciting. Also, like Socrates, he always had his cults of students at his heels. I especially like the picture that Plato leaves of Protagoras, meditating in his garden, with his students following in single-file behind him, their arms folded behind their backs as his were, and also like him, making a U-turn when coming to the end of the garden and then falling into line again.

Jansson was one of his cult of young, worshipful rangers whom he had carefully selected to be his eyes. They were to check for facts while he spun theories. Jansson was one of the cult selected to see whether fire whirls always moved in a clockwise motion. It was a great honor to have been selected to observe fire whirls—probably no spectacular phenomenon of nature had ever been less studied close-up, for the simple reason that those few throughout history who had a chance to see a fire whirl managed to survive it by getting as far away from it as was rapidly possible.

On the day of the fire, while the smokejumpers were coming down gulch to get to the safety of the river at its mouth, Jansson was coming up gulch trying to locate the smokejumpers whose radio and connection with the outside world had been shattered when the radio's parachute had not opened. Coming upgulch, Jansson walked right into the vortex of the fire whirl that ignited the tragic blowup. He fainted from lack of oxygen in the breathless center of the vortex and himself almost became the first victim of the Mann Gulch fire. On November 9, as he and Gisborne worked their way down the gulch, Gisborne began to doubt whether a fire whirl and a blowup had caused the Mann Gulch tragedy—he was still too far upgulch to see where the fire whirl had begun, but we can already get a glimpse of the scientific relation between the founder of your science and his first worshipful students. He began to give Jansson a kidding lesson on keeping his observations detached and independent of authority, even his. This exciting man may have had a dash of Shelley and Socrates in him, but in the showdown he was the hard-nosed son of a logger looking for facts that were often marks on trees. He didn't see the right marks, and, when he didn't, he began to kid his devoted student, almost succeeding in persuading him that there had been no fire whirl in Mann Gulch although Jansson had almost died in one.

To get the feeling of this last day in Mann Gulch you must also get more of a feeling for Jansson, his worshipful student. You must also be able to visualize the literary form in which the worshipful student cast his insurance report. The large part of it consists of a listing of 37 of what the report refers to as "Rest Stops." At each "Rest Stop," starting from the first to the last, there is a brief designation of the subject of conversation that occurred there plus usually a direct quotation of some "pertinent remark" made by Gisborne at that spot. The literary form is much like what a worshipful disciple would use if he were accompanying his master through the stations of the cross, only instead of being 14 stations there were, as I said, 37 "Rest Stops." At station 29, Gisborne said to his selected observer of fire whirls who recently had almost been killed by one: "I don't believe your fire whirled. You only thought so because of what you have been told, by me in part." So great was his student's devotion that he himself began to doubt he had fainted and then vomited when he reached the river. "That's true—" he said, "I suppose I could have interpreted my observations wrong, but after I got out of the fire I observed two distinct whirls."

They continued downgulch to station 32. Notice who sees first. Gisborne: "Look here—what's this?" Jansson: "That's my whirl!" Gisborne: "Yep—it follows right around the ridge. What we really should do now to really complete the job is to follow it out."

It went straight toward Hellman's cross. The slope there is 76 degrees—almost perpendicular. It was at the end of a long, and, for Jansson, a very frightening day, and he became more frightened as Gisborne insisted they map the uphill course of the fire whirl. At first Gisborne argued with his student just as if he had been told he couldn't climb the 150 foot dead spruce at Priest River. With all his toughness, though, this man of many colors must have had a wide band of human sensitivity. Suddenly, he seemed to realize that, although he himself had no fear of death, Jansson would never forgive himself if anything bad happened to him in Mann Gulch. Suddenly, he was very contrite and apologetic, but not until Jansson promised him that he himself would return to Mann Gulch before winter and map the lines of the fire whirl.

They sidehilled out of Mann Gulch. At stop 35 Gisborne said: "Well, this was a nice way to come back. I made it okay. I'm glad I got a chance to get up here. Tomorrow we can get all our dope together and work on Hypothesis #1. Maybe it will lead to a theory."

In my story of the Mann Gulch fire, the chapter on the rescue of its dead crew ends with a short account of the death of Harry Gisborne. I should like to conclude by reading the last page of it.

They were following a game trail along the cliffs high above the Missouri River in the lower end of the Gates of the Mountains, and were only a quarter or a half mile from their truck when they reached Stop 37. Gisborne says: "Here's a nice place to sit and watch the river. I made it good. My legs might ache a little though tomorrow."

In his report Jansson says: "I think Gisborne's rising at point 37 on the map was due to the attack hitting him." He goes on to explain in parentheses that "Thrombosis cases usually want to stand or sit up because of difficulty in breathing." Gisborne died within a minute and Jansson piled rocks high around him so he would not roll off the game trail into the Missouri River 100 feet below.

When Jansson knew Gisborne was dead, he stretched him out straight on the game trail, built the rocks higher around him, closed his eyes, and then put his glasses back on his eyes so, if he woke up, he could see where he was.

Then Jansson ran for help. The stars came out. The great Missouri repeated the same succession of chords in passing the cliffs below that it likely will to eternity. The only other motion was the moon floating across the lens of Gisborne's glasses, which at last were unobservant. Nothing moved on the game trail.

This is the death of a scientist, a scientist who did much to establish a science. On the day of his death he had the pleasure of discovering two of his theories were wrong. On the day of his death he was correct—his theory that fire whirls always rotate clockwise was in error and his theory about the cause of the Mann Gulch blowup was also probably wrong.

It would be revealing if tomorrow had come and he had got all his "dope" together and had worked out Hypothesis #1. Maybe it would have led to another theory, probably the right one.

This is the way for a scientist to live and die—maybe the ideal way for any of us to—excitedly finding we were wrong and excitedly waiting for tomorrow to come so we can start over again, get our dope together again, and find Hypothesis #1.

Even without his theory of tomorrow, but in part because of him, we are now able to form what is likely the correct theory. I am one who should hope so.

In any event, I thank you for inviting me back to my hometown and for giving me a chance to talk to you about a man I met in Mann Gulch.

Interviews

The Two Worlds of
Norman Maclean:
Interviews
in Montana and Chicago

William Kittredge and Annick Smith*

During the summer of 1983, Norman Maclean met with William Kittredge and Annick Smith several times to discuss the possibility of making a film based on his novel, A River Runs Through It. *Although the three had met before, these summer meetings in Montana—at Maclean's cabin on Seeley Lake, Smith's house in the Blackfoot Valley, and Kittredge's apartment in Missoula—drew them together for hours of storytelling over country dinners and Wild Turkey. Probing for autobiographical material for the film script, and simply hoping to record Maclean's stories, Kittredge and Smith asked Maclean for an interview. The Montana part of the interview was taped at Kittredge's place in early September, just before Maclean drove back to Chicago after his annual Montana summer sojourn. A month later, Smith visited her parents in Chicago and stopped for lunch with Maclean at the Quadrangle Club at the University of Chicago, learning to her surprise that he had once managed the faculty club for a year, bringing it out of the red and leaving it with a solid profit. After a walk around campus (Smith had been a student at the College during the fifties), they returned to Maclean's home on Woodlawn Avenue and*

*"The Two Worlds of Norman Maclean" by William Kittredge and Annick Smith is reprinted from *TriQuarterly 60* (Spring/Summer 1984), pp. 412-432. Copyright © 1984 by William Kittredge and Annick Smith. *TriQuarterly* is a publication of Northwestern University. Reprinted with the permission of the authors and the publisher.

recorded the Chicago portion of the interview. What follows is a condensed version of these conversations in Montana and Chicago.

TQ: I imagine you'd say fishing is the best game.

MACLEAN: Oh, I wouldn't say so. But I thought it was, for a while in my life. My family, which was British and Scotch and reserved in the expression of its emotions, especially in any emotions about loving, didn't talk about how much we loved each other. It would have been unthinkable. But fishing was the one place where we could say how much we admired one another. We could also talk about how much we didn't like some things. I'd tell my brother, "Ah, you played that fish like a Chinaman—God Almighty."

I couldn't think of saying such a thing to him normally. Fishing is where we all opened our hearts, including my mother. And I think that's the greatest thing that fishing still does. Now I fish alone, but I don't fish the best water any more; I fish where I used to fish with my brother, where my brother and I fished as a family— when I go fishing it's a memorial to my family. So I don't fish alone. Fishing in our family was science, religion, and grace—and rhythm was very important. Somehow the universe is rhythmical. When you're good you get in touch with the universe by catching its rhythms. My father taught me to cast on a four-count beat, with a metronome. I wasn't kidding when I said that in my family there was no clear line between religion and fly fishing.

My father had a great sense of artistry. If you made beauty you had it made with my Protestant father. He played with grace, with the word itself. It always had some kind of religious implication, even if it was nothing more than graceful casting. He thought that was a kind of religious manifestation. My father preached twice on Sunday and he would be all wound up after his morning service and I would walk with him. When we lived on the north side of Missoula we'd walk up to the waterworks reservoir on the hill, or maybe up Rattlesnake Creek. When we lived across the Clark Fork we'd walk up the Milwaukee Railroad tracks to Spring Gulch. And he used to say to me, "Son, I want you to know that when you get old enough to go to college, I'll have enough money saved so that you can go to any college in the world that you're able to get into." I cannot tell you what that assurance did to my character. He made $1,800 a year and what he saved, he saved out of that. His saying what he and my mother were going to do for me was one of the most important things in my life.

TQ: So you could go to Dartmouth if you wanted.

MACLEAN: But I almost started out at Harvard.

TQ: But you were seriously considering devoting your life to being a forest ranger.

MACLEAN: My father did not allow me to start elementary school but taught me himself. Most everything crucial that happened to me since has been influenced by his teaching. He was a very stern teacher, very harsh. He put me in a room across from his, where he worked every morning on his sermons while my mother ran the church. I'd study for forty-five minutes and then I'd recite to him for fifteen. He might start me off in the morning by telling me to write a theme on such and such. All I got was writing and reading, nothing else. So I would write this thing and three-quarters of an hour later I would bring it in to him, and he'd tear it apart and say take it back and write it half the length. So I'd take it back with tears in my eyes. It was rough, this kind of treatment, learning economy of style when kids my age were learning their ABC's. So I'd give it back to him, and he'd say, "O.K., now do it half as long again," so I'd take it back and do it again and by that time it would be a quarter of twelve, and he'd say, now throw it away.

Then we'd go fishing, or we'd go to the ball game. There was a great minor league in Montana, Idaho, and Utah in those days, the Union League. It had some very, very great baseball players, Bullet Joe Bush, Walter Johnson, some of the very best on their way up.

We had a season ticket, and after the games we would go out to the woods, or else I would go alone.

I came very early to love Wordsworth. My father had what was called Family Worship, reading to us after breakfast and after supper. He read to us from the Bible, or religious poets such as Milton and Wordsworth. Which ties up with the lonely life I was leading. Very early I got the sense that this was a complete life—terrific intellectual discipline half the day, and freedom, nature, doing what I wanted to do, the world of baseball and sports, hunting and fishing, the other half. I didn't realize it was schizophrenia coming.

When I saw that's what was coming, I said, that's what's coming, but it is not going to be schizophrenia for me. I'm going to see that I live two lives as one life—clear to the end. So all the years when I was teaching at the University of Chicago, come summer when all the big scholars were going over to the British Museum, standing outside talking to each other and letting the pigeons shit on them from the roof, I was out here in Montana. I knew one thing—in the summer get back to Montana.

TQ: In those days, did you share this kind of roaming with your brother, Paul, or was he too much younger?

MACLEAN: He was much younger—three years. We got split apart early because I started in the Forest Service early. For a kid I got to be a kind of prodigy in the woods. World War I came and they had a foolish draft in which they immediately took the best men out of the Forest Service. Where could they get better men? So in the woods they had to turn immediately to old bastards or young punks like me. When I was fourteen I was working way over on the Selway and the Lochsa, a couple of the worst spots in the Northwest. And I worked for the Forest Service through my undergraduate years and my first two years of teaching at Dartmouth—right up until I got a job at the University of Chicago.

That was my last year in the woods for the Forest Service, and when I came out I was kind of mature, but I made a miscalculation. I thought the work was going always to be horses and walking. I'd lose twenty or twenty-five pounds every summer, and end up weighing only 125 pounds. I'd look at myself in the mirror and my cheeks were just big hollows. And I thought, here I am, in this shape when I'm young and tough. If I keep this up, it's going to kill me. But as it turned out, pretty soon they had a road up every gulch, and they had four-wheel drives and helicopters and Christ knows what else. You can't go from your office to your toilet in the Forest Service now—unless you go in a jeep.

I just figured I better quit while I could.

TQ: Why, then, after two years of teaching at Dartmouth, did you leave school and come back to the Forest Service in Helena? After you thought you'd quit that life for good?

MACLEAN: My father was a strange and wonderful guy. He allowed me great freedom, but he must have known a lot about me. He let me go my own way, which is very Scotch in the most elevated sense. He knew that as a teacher what you wanted to do was make your student independent of yourself.

My father never asked me about how things were going at Dartmouth, and I never made much comment, but after my second year of teaching there, when I came back, he said to me in a kind of offhand way, "I don't think you've learned much this year." And that really sunk me, because I knew it was true. That year I'd kept on hanging around with some poker-playing pals who still hadn't graduated. I had made quite a reputation as a teacher, but I didn't admire myself.

That was late August, and I thought, "Christ, I didn't learn anything this year. And I don't see where I'm going." So I wrote the chairman of the English Department, who was a great admirer of mine—must have been the eighth or tenth of September—and I asked if he could get somebody to take my classes, because I didn't think I ought to go back any more. And I told him why.

TQ: That was in 1926, and you were working on a Master of Arts at Dartmouth?

MACLEAN: Nothing. I was taking the boys at poker.

TQ: Your father was in Helena at this time?

MACLEAN: Yes, he had become the leader of the Presbyterian Church in Montana, and Helena is the capital.

TQ: The time of *A River Runs Through It* is not real time, is it?

MACLEAN: Not exactly. Your life makes movements that don't have any artistic merit.

TQ: So you gave up teaching?

MACLEAN: My father had great influence on me. And I had great doubts about whether teaching was what I wanted to do. I had always had this strong attraction to the Forest Service, and for not the best of reasons—reasons that turned out to be not particularly valid. Eventually I quit the Forest Service for good, and went back to the University of Chicago with a teaching assistantship, and taught and took my degree at the same time. But that was two years later.

TQ: Paul went to Dartmouth too, didn't he? Two years at the University of Montana and two at Dartmouth?

MACLEAN: 1927 and 1928.

TQ: So, when you quit teaching at Dartmouth and came back to Helena to work for the Forest Service again, he went to Dartmouth.

MACLEAN: My father couldn't support both of us east at school at the same time. When Paul got to go, there was something funny that happened. To enter, we had to have four years of Latin, four years of math, four years of English. Paul didn't have the four years of high-school math. He entered Dartmouth as a junior, and he should have made up his math deficiency that year, but he didn't. When he wasn't called on it that year, he figured he had them by the balls—they couldn't stop him in his senior year and make him go back and take high-school math. And sure enough he got almost all the way to his degree. I was in Montana then, and I got this telegram: "I can't get out of this damned place because I never got in."

Dartmouth settled with him, telling him he would have to take a university math course at the University of Montana over the summer. They had a great math teacher at UM in those days, Nels Johann Lennes. A very distinguished guy, who wrote college and high-school texts. Lennes was also a real political radical. My brother made it clear that he was, too. They spent their time in class defiling the Anaconda Mining Company.

Paul got a big grade in the course and his degree. I came out of the Forest Service to celebrate and I decided we would have a convocation for Paul in Missoula. I got all his drunken friends and a couple just out of prison, and we went over to the church and stole a few choir gowns for the night, and had all these thugs in choir gowns. We marched down Higgins Avenue, and I got up and gave the convocation speech at the corner of Higgins and Front streets, and my friends say it was my best-made piece of prose ever.

TQ: What did your father think of all that?

MACLEAN: If it didn't get too rough, he liked it. He'd come in to me on a Sunday morning, after I had been in a big fight Saturday night, and he would look at me all covered with blood and shake me, and he'd say, "How did you come off last night?" And if I said, "Well, I won," he would say, "Good, take it easy—sleep it off." But if I said, "Well, I lost," it'd be, "Get out of bed and over to church! Shame on you!"

TQ: Your mother, how did she feel about all this?

MACLEAN: Well, my mother, she was a special case. She handled a man's world all about her. It was a tough world for her, she and three men—and they trying hard to be men, too. She handled us with great power, and in part by just not concerning herself with our efforts to be men.

She and my father fought for my soul when I was young, my father wanting me to be a tough guy and my mother wanting me to be a flower girl. So I ended being a tough flower girl. She had a lot of influence on me. In a lot of ways I was closer to her than to my father. And I certainly look more like her. He was redheaded.

TQ: Did she have a special affection for Paul, too?

MACLEAN: Yes, she had a special affection for Paul. It seemed that the worse sinners we were, the more she loved us. It wasn't that she tried to protect us from ourselves, because she just acted as though we did no sin. But she had a great affection for Paul. He was so kidding, and made love to her so openly, gave her big hugs. He'd lean right back and hold her and laugh at her. She loved it. No man in her life had ever made love to her like that.

TQ: To get back to chronology, during the years that you are talking about in *A River Runs Through It*, right before your brother's death, you were still coming home to Montana for the summer?

MACLEAN: That's right. I always do. I always have.

TQ: What year did you get married?

MACLEAN: 1931. I waited until I got more or less a full-time job teaching at the University of Chicago, a full instructorship.

TQ: You told us a story the other day about meeting your wife.

MACLEAN: That was in '26 or '27 when I met Jessie. It was in the winter in a big snowstorm on a sheep ranch that now belongs to the Baucus family, up Canyon Creek. It was before Christmas, because we came up there not expecting trouble with the weather, and this monster came. My partner, who was a great driver, had to drive home, with him and me and my future wife and his woman in my wife's car. We got out there on the plains in the Helena valley and the radiator froze and in a little while the engine overheated and the car quit.

TQ: So you were stuck out there?

MACLEAN: Stuck. I got out and walked about three or four miles in the blizzard to town, and when I got home I did a foolish thing. I got a bucket of warm water, took it out and poured it in the radiator of our family car. The car was in the garage, and of course it had been drained for the winter. I poured that water into the radiator, and the moment it hit the radiator, it froze solid. I was right where I started, only worse. So I started walking back to her car. I could see my partner and those two women freezing in the blizzard. But I only got part way out when I met them coming in. The engine had cooled, so they started it. Her radiator was frozen solid, but it was so cold outside the engine kept going until we got home. I had to work two or three months to pay for it. It was really in terrible shape. So that's how I met my wife.

TQ: There's another story you tell about your courtship. How you proposed to your wife.

MACLEAN: That was the next spring—in June, the big flood month. I don't think I saw her very much during the couple of months I worked paying for the car. I wasn't happily disposed, I guess. But in spring she invited me to come to her place with her for a weekend. It was a great honor and sought by all the young guys around. It was a Scotch-Irish family and very, very hospitable. They made a point of making everyone feel joyous and glad to be there, and they ran a big hospitable table.

Jessie worked in Helena in an accounting office. She was a CPA— a very good one. So we took her car, a Studebaker, and we started off in June to go down to Wolf Creek. That canyon is a narrow canyon, like plenty of places in Montana, like the Blackfoot River canyon, only more so. There's not room in the bottom of the canyon for a road, a railroad, and the river. That's Prickly Pear Canyon. Once in a while, when that situation occurred, the railroad went up high and ran along the side of the cliffs and went through a railroad tunnel.

Well, when we got to the canyon, the goddamned canyon was flooded with spring runoff and shortly we couldn't move forward. So she backed up high, where the railroad and the road separated, and the railroad stayed up high and went through a tunnel and across this bridge and finally connected with the road again. So we backed up to where the railroad took off and then she turned and went through the guard with the car, and over the ties and into the tunnel. And I said, "Christ, you're not going in there with the car, are you?" Because, you know, the Great Northern line was operating full blast through there then, always hauling ore from Butte to the smelter in Great Falls, and freight trains can come through at any time. She said, "Sure. I know when the trains come." And I said, "You don't know when a freight train will come—freight will come whenever there's a trainload." But anyway, we went through.

The next year, a road crew was working in that same tunnel, and a train came through and plastered them on the walls. I fell in love with her on the way through, but I wasn't happy, and when we came out, here was this trestle going over the Prickly Pear far down below. I wasn't in the best psychological state when I looked down through those ties and saw that goddamned little silvery trickle. It seemed a mile away. We drove across that trestle and almost immediately afterwards we connected again with the main road.

So she got back on the main road and stopped her motor. I told her, "You know, I'm pretty impressed with the way you drive that car. Some day I might ask you to marry me." And she said, "Well, you better get used to high places before you do."

TQ: You said she was Irish?

MACLEAN: Scotch-Irish. Her mother was a Scot from Nova Scotia, and her father was an Irishman.

TQ: What did they do? Were they ranchers?

MACLEAN: No, they ran the big store. It sold everything and was the only store in town.

TQ: How long after that did you propose to her?

MACLEAN: Not too long. I was really impressed. She always had that offhand reckless style. I'd say, "I don't know if we've got enough money to do something or other." She'd say, "How much do we have in the bank?" So I'd tell her, "We've got some," and she said, "If we've got some, we've got plenty."

TQ: How did she get along with Paul?

MACLEAN: They respected one another and became great friends. Paul was working on the Helena paper. In those days there were two Helena papers, an evening and a daily paper, both owned by the ACM, and he worked on both. They had a wonderful tough editor name of Bill Campbell, a famous tough son of a bitch, a great vitriolic writer who specialized in castrating the members of the Helena congregation. Every day he'd cut the balls off somebody. My brother liked that. So my brother and Bill Campbell were very close and admired each other greatly, while everybody in town hated them.

They depended heavily on their families, as such guys often do. With all their brutality, they were very tender to their families, and depended heavily on the support and tenderness of the family since they got nothing from the outside world which resembled warmth and admiration. There was a big streak of the adversary in my brother. He was taking on the world all the time, and so was Campbell. It was their great joy.

TQ: Do you think that accounts for Paul's gambling?

MACLEAN: I really don't know. I think there are things you allow yourself and your family that are beyond human understanding. But I don't think gambling is much out of the normal. When it came to fishing, though, my brother admitted nobody could touch him, just nobody. Fishing for him was an elegant sport and all that, but essentially fishing was getting fish and beating the other guy. Anything to beat him!

TQ: Like throwing rocks in the river?

MACLEAN: Yes. I'd get out of the car, and take my time, and put my rod together and kind of look around and breathe the ozone. He'd be fishing fifteen or twenty minutes before I got a fly on the water. That was always his theory. "Brother," he'd say, "you can't catch a fish with your fly in the air."

TQ: Seems Paul and your wife were a lot alike, both of them feeling great confidence as they moved through the world.

MACLEAN: Oh, yes. She came back to Chicago before we got married. I said, "We can't get married now. I've already made my sortie out into space and returned empty-handed, without knowing what I'm going to do. I can't try that again. I can't go back there and get married. I'd have to spend my time making a living. I've got to get my degree."

"Oh, that's fine," she said. "I'll come back, and I'll work." And she did. "I'll work until we can be married." So that was that, and she worked until she died. Some of our happiest years I think were before we got married.

TQ: What did Jessie Maclean look like?

MACLEAN: Well, my wife was very Scotch—redheaded, freckle-faced, the kind of freckles that go with red hair. Thin, strong, fast, her heels clicked when she walked. She had a kind of style about her, she had what I called "swish." We were very different. I was always the romantic, she was the realist.

I was always moaning around about the passing of youth, how life was over at twenty-one. Once she got tired of always hearing me moaning, and finally she said, "Norman, I knew you when you were young, and you were a goddamned mess."

TQ: What years were your children born?

MACLEAN: Well, my daughter was forty her last birthday, and my son is a year younger.

TQ: So they were born during World War II. Did you ever regret raising them in Chicago instead of Montana?

MACLEAN: In this matter, as in so many others, it's hard for me to know what my attitudes were. My wife had so much influence in shaping my stance about life. She was western—in many ways more western than I was. But she would scold me about the fact that I rejected a lot of Chicago scenery and customs and was always looking for places that looked like Montana, and we'd go out walking in the country often and she'd tell me, "You don't treat Chicago with the kindness that you treat Montana. I don't know what you expect."

I knew Montana history. There wasn't any part of the scenery that wasn't enriched by knowledge of some kind. But I didn't know a damned thing about Illinois, which is one of the richest states in the Union in its history. And she'd say, "You know, you've got to try to take the great eccentricities of the place you are in and make the most of them. So we aren't making any money, but I'll tell you when we have children, they're all going to the University schools from nursery school to Ph.D. I don't care if I have to scrub on my knees to pay. That's one of the great compensations that we have— that we've been blessed with a great educational system accessible for our children." That was her prevailing and constant attitude about things and I have tried to make it mine, not always success-fully.

When I first came here, obviously I didn't feel this way or she wouldn't have been scolding me about my being resistant to finding anything to like about Chicago and Chicagoans. But I've come to love Chicago, and I think—I know—she gave me the original impulse to do that.

TQ: With your own family, didn't you need a kind of a game like fishing in order to get the same closeness? . . . I'm talking about your own children.

MACLEAN: Oh, well, they never . . . I had just the boy and a girl. No, my daughter one time was a fine fisherman and a good caster. She loves the outdoors and is still a good caster. But my son is a great fisherman. He's one of the finest fisherman, I'm sure, of his generation and in a way in which none of us are, because a lot of his life has been in the East and he's become a master of fishing in the East. He knows where the trout are there. He's a master of fishing in Vermont and Maine. The rest of us don't even know where to fish there.

TQ: Around Chicago, though, you couldn't do much fishing.

MACLEAN: No, I never have tried. No.

TQ: Is there anything in the city that took that place for you?

MACLEAN: Well, there must have been. Of course my family was all split up by then because my father and mother lived in Montana and died there. So that family, at least, became dead or distant. My new family—my wife and my own children—never centered around fishing.

TQ: What did you center around?

MACLEAN: In many ways we didn't center, and that's kind of a sad part of my life. My children were growing up during the war, and I just didn't have any time for them when they were young— or any energy. I was exhausted all the time, taking more things on and scheduling more.

TQ: How did the war affect you?

MACLEAN: I enlisted in Naval Aviation. Largely because the great football player Jay Berwanger was in there and he and I were great pals and he wanted me to come in. I enlisted, but then the University requested that I be not accepted. So I stayed here, and tried to do five or ten different jobs.

TQ: What were some of the five or ten?

MACLEAN: Well, I tried to teach a full schedule in English. I was the Dean of Students in the college. I was also in charge of Naval recruitment on campus. We started a voluntary program for military training called the Institute of Military Studies, and it was a very good thing for the early years of the war. We put through about ten thousand men. Nobody knew anything about the military in this country and if you got in the Army and knew something— even left foot from right foot—you advanced rapidly, and the guys needed money if they were going in, especially those who were married. So we had this circus going on every night of the week and also on Saturday and Sunday, giving basic military training, and also military specializations in language or code-breaking or whatnot or rifle shooting. And so when I became director of the Institute I did that at night, and often I ran the rifle range. I didn't have any time. It's a real sorrow of mine. I feel that I never picked up my children at the age when I should have. I was tired all the time.

TQ: A lot of things changed at the University right after the war when all the veterans came back on the GI Bill. Do you want to talk a little bit about that?

MACLEAN: Well, I don't remember that very well. I guess I was just glad the goddamned war was over. I don't have very many memories of it—that wasn't a very important period in my life. When the war was over, I guess I just rested for a while.

TQ: Have you ever written anything about Chicago?

MACLEAN: When I retired, I started writing. When I started writing, I started writing about the University of Chicago, and some of the nicest things and kindest things I believe I've ever written were short pieces that were published in the alumni magazine. God, I even did one on Albert Michelson, the first American scientist to win the Nobel Prize, whom I used to play billiards with.

TQ: Where did you and Michelson play?

MACLEAN: Over at the faculty club. The billiard room is on the first floor. I think that was one of the finest things I ever wrote. I got over five hundred letters in response.

Michelson was a strange and wonderful man—and a great billiard player. Once when he ran about thirty-five and missed he shook his head and said, "I'm not what I used to be." And I said, "You know, you're a great billiard player still." And he said, "Well, billiards is a good game," then he said, "but billiards isn't as good a game as chess," and then he said, "but chess isn't as good a game as physics." He had artistry in everything he did. You know, he was a violin maker and a painter.

I was just a young punk and he was the first Nobel Prize winner in science in our country. These days Nobel Prize winners are a dime a dozen, but in that day, he was *it*. He and Einstein were the two outstanding scientists in the world. I still think they are great.

TQ: When you first came to Chicago from Montana, what were some of your feelings about the place, coming from the West as a westerner?

MACLEAN: No matter what first question you ask me about Chicago, I ought to answer by saying that usually what I mean by Chicago is a town of about forty- or fifty-thousand, with the big city not entirely inaccessible, but not easy to get to, and one I frequent very, very infrequently. Surrounded by a wonderful park system designed by the great landscape architect Frederick Law Olmstead—you know, he had his hand in that as well as in the World's Fair. I think one of the prizes of Chicago is the great park system in it and around it, with the lake on the other side. So my life here has been largely the University and Hyde Park. I get to town for the August and January sales. But my life is most deeply connected with the University, and I try—I tried even when I was teaching—to get out to the parks two or three times a week. Now that I'm retired, I try to get out there more frequently than that.

TQ: You were telling me a little while ago, when we visited Rockefeller Chapel, that when you first arrived here they were putting up the bells.

MACLEAN: By the time the bells were going up, there was this very deep feeling of despair and anger from the Depression that had come to the surface. The bells were unloaded there on Woodlawn and would stand sometimes a week or more before they were hoisted up into the tower. The people gathered there in the evenings were very, very bitter. They were embittered by Rockefeller and the University, and especially by all this useless display of money spent for things that rang at night. They couldn't really make themselves at home where their home was. I remember it vividly—the kind of despair of the Depression that came to the surface there. You wouldn't see it often, either in town or when I went back to Montana. I think most people try to cover up their feelings about the despair they are going through. It's silent in Hammond now. But the bells made them vocal. Possibly because they were Rockefeller's bells.

TQ: What year was that?

MACLEAN: Well, I came to Chicago in '28. Possibly '30 or '31. I was a graduate student and also immediately a part-time teacher called a graduate assistant—a form of degradation that's since been abolished. In English we all taught Compulsory Composition, got paid $200 a section, maybe about thirty to thirty-five students in a section, and we would teach three sections a quarter and then try to be graduate students working for a Ph.D. That way we made $600 a quarter—$1,800 a year—and managed to survive.

TQ: That was about the sum your father made.

MACLEAN: That's what my father made as a minister. These were really very desperate times and we had to work desperately hard. I'll never forget how hard we worked. We had about sixty papers to correct a week, and in those days they thought you couldn't learn to write unless often you wrote a long thing. So each student would write two papers a week—one a thousand words and one five hundred. The professors were shocked when I asked them why have regular long papers, and they said, "Well, you couldn't tell whether a student could organize unless he had a big thing to write." I told them, "You show me a paragraph of a student, and I'll tell you whether he can write or think." None of us teaching composition was happy. You'd come home with all those papers on the weekend and have a few drinks and sit around and try to talk. And then you'd go to bed and start grading papers, and never get out of bed until Monday morning, when it was time to go back to teaching and talking again. I was too tired to get out of bed until I had to teach.

TQ: Was Robert M. Hutchins at Chicago when you first arrived?

MACLEAN: Oh, he came here around '29, as I remember—the year after I came, when he was thirty. He got his show started in '31, when the new college began. That's when I quit teaching English Composition and started teaching the Humanities course, and

I became an instructor at a pretty good salary. That's when Jessie and I got married, in '31.

TQ: How did you feel about being in that kind of atmosphere after coming from Montana?

MACLEAN: I thought it was high-gear, but I felt in some ways very much at home. In a lot of ways, the people here are more western than western people. There's always this myth about western people being free and independent, easy and honest of speech and so on. But I found that to be truer about the people of the University of Chicago than I did about the people of any other place I've ever lived in. I can talk straight to them. They talk straight to me. There are a lot of people at the University of Chicago who say what they mean.

One of the western things about the University when I came here was that there wasn't this strict social and economic stratification of society according to whether you're an instructor or an assistant professor or an associate or a full professor. And that was especially noticeable to me because I'd come from Dartmouth where this kind of stratification was very, very prominent—especially in the English Department, because the chairman of that department, although in many ways a really fine person, was still very English. When we were invited up to his place for dinner, we were invited as instructors and there wasn't any other class of society around, and furthermore, we all had to wear tuxedos. I don't think I've had a tuxedo on since I've been in Chicago. The result of that is that I made some wondrous friends as a young man in Chicago, including Michelson. A barefoot boy from the banks of the Blackfoot River, having as a friend the first American Nobel Prize winner in science.

TQ: Who were some of your more literary friends?

MACLEAN: Another of my dear friends was Ferdinand Schevill, who had been an early member of the faculty and a great historian and a vivid and wonderful character—a great storyteller, and very learned, his specialty being Florence, Italy. He had such a vivid personality that he had a universal circle of friends of a literary nature. He himself had a summer home in the dunes just north of Michigan City, where many university faculty had homes or spent the weekend. They'd take the Yellow Peril out there to Michigan City and then walk or have a bicycle and ride twenty-five or thirty miles.

He had formed a great friendship with Carl Sandburg and Sherwood Anderson. Of course, it was still the time when Chicago was one of the great literary centers of the world. The real guys were here in those days and not in New York or some other place. So two of his great friends were Sandburg and Sherwood Anderson, and he was closely associated with Sandburg from his University of Chicago days. In those days there was a great interlacing between faculty and literary and artistic guys in Chicago that there isn't now. It was really a more solid community. So he knew Sandburg well and Sandburg had this place out in the dunes area, built right into the sand dunes with these goats, you know, on the roof of his place and the sand coming down, and the goats would go up there and graze—a kind of strange and wonderful place. And Ferdinand would take me along with him.

Now Schevill and Sherwood Anderson were great friends also, but Sherwood had great contempt for Sandburg. He thought he was a kind of moaner, and not a writer, getting by saying m-m-m-m-m, the way he read his poetry—kind of in a singsong way. He just didn't rate Sandburg as a writer at all, and thought he was full of crap. On the other hand, Ferdinand and Sherwood had this fixed friendship—partly based on both of them thinking they were great croquet players. Sherwood was running that newspaper in West Virginia and Ferdinand would go to West Virginia and they'd have these croquet tournaments, and they kept a regular inventory of their games year after year. They would change places and Sherwood would come to see Ferdinand in Chicago. They were very careful to take turns.

So it was Sherwood's turn and he was going to come up here and have his round of croquet games. I was invited out to Ferdinand's and Sherwood was there, and Sherwood would say, "Well, I suppose we'll have to go up and listen to that old bullshitter tonight." That meant Sandburg. And Ferdinand said, "You know, you shouldn't feel . . . he doesn't feel that way about you . . . he'd be horrified." And Sherwood said, "I'll go up there." But he wasn't very happy about it.

So up we go, after the day was over, to Sandburg's home, and we come in the door on a little platform that was higher than the floor of the main room. So we came in and Sherwood just stopped and froze and looked at Sandburg. Sandburg is engaged in one of his monologues. So he's mooning along about Emerson, the first really great true American. And Sherwood listens for a while. Finally he stops Sandburg right in the middle of a sentence. He says, "Emerson was the first great Rotarian." Boom. The place just froze. There we stood, up on the platform like actors, with a stunned audience beneath us. Well, there was no more to the evening at all. Nobody could get anything started after that.

So, a couple of days later, I'm going in to Chicago and Ferdinand takes me down to Michigan City, and I got on the Yellow Peril. Who's sitting in the Yellow Peril but Sandburg. You know, with his snap-brim hat and his long thin cigar. So I go over and sit by him and he looks at me for a while and he doesn't say a word. Then he says, "That sorry . . . that son of a bitch!" he said. "What does he mean? What does he mean about Emerson being the first great Rotarian?" He pulled the brim of his hat down until it touched his cigar and never said another word to me all the way to Chicago. All was not quiet on the Chicago literary front in those days.

TQ: What was the Yellow Peril?

MACLEAN: It was that South Bend train . . . it is yellow, and it's sure a peril. That's what everybody called it that used it in those days—the Yellow Peril.

Maybe if I talk long enough you would realize in some particular area what I mean when I said that in many ways Chicago, for a young unknown kid from the West, was more western than the

West. There's a kind of fundamental, inhibited politeness about western people to prevent them from being class-free. I found Chicago class-free, and I have ever since I've been here. I have never felt that anybody was pulling class on me or social privilege. I've really lived a life almost devoid of social superiors, and I resent anything like that or anything that I think comes close to that.

For instance, I spent a lot of time in Boston when I went to Dartmouth because I didn't have money enough to go home on vacations and I had a lot of relatives in Boston. I expected them to be very snooty and all stiff-laced—all that stuff about Boston. They were very warm and generous to me. They recognized that I was different in a way in which people in Chicago didn't. In Chicago, we seemed to be about the same kind of people, but in Boston I was recognized as different from them, and so far as I had differences with them, they accepted those differences.

TQ: Do you think Chicago is still class-free?

MACLEAN: Well, it's hard for me to tell. In the years since I retired I wanted to write a few things before I died. I've had to give up many things. I've had to give up friends and society and a lot of the time that I normally would have spent with people, so I don't know. My guess is, no, it hasn't changed much. A Scotch poet would say, "A man's a man for a' that and a' that and a' that."

TQ: Do you think that cuts across racial lines as well?

MACLEAN: Yes, I'm almost devoid of racial feeling, and I feel fortunate.

TQ: I didn't mean you, personally, I meant the openness of the city.

MACLEAN: No, the city in some ways has aspects of ethnic growth much like Canada's, for instance, where each ethnic group has really been encouraged—not merely permitted but encouraged—to retain its Russian or Yugoslavian nature. There's some of that here. I found it very warm-hearted as a city. The Italians are warm-hearted, the Jews are warm-hearted. The Irish are in some ways the snootiest of all, the most inbred. They really can do without you, except your vote. But I'm very happy about the relations I've had with the different ethnic groups. I'm happy, too, that they cook so well.

TQ: Did you ever go to some of the jazz places on the South Side?

MACLEAN: When I first came here, you know, it was the center of black migration from the South—right across the park. Some of the greatest jazz outfits ever put together played there. They didn't go all the way into the Loop station. They were riding the rods and they'd get arrested if they rode all the way into the Loop. So there was a station here at Sixty-third. They'd roll off at Sixty-third Street. You can't believe the great jazz musicians we had. Saturday nights we'd all go walking across the park. We had a gang. Even then, people never walked across the parks alone. We'd get a gang and go over there. And they tell me it's good again, some really good outfits over there, but I'm too old to care.

TQ: What are some of your favorite city pastimes?

MACLEAN: I just told you.

TQ: Right. Eating ethnic food, going to parks, playing billiards, jazz. What about team sports? You used to go to baseball games in Missoula. What about here?

MACLEAN: Here we're right near the Sox park, and very early I became a Sox fan. In those days the games didn't start until three o'clock. So you could teach a one-thirty or two o'clock class and get out there in time to see most of the ball game. So Bob Streeter and I went to a lot of ball games—a lot more than I do now, since the games have been changed to one-thirty or at night. Bob is a very learned baseball fan. He went to college at Bucknell, and that's where the great Christy Mathewson started pitching. When the "Round Table" was still a national radio program, Bob and I and Bill Veeck were on a program together. It was a very good program.

TQ: In those days Chicago had quite a football team, too, didn't it?

MACLEAN: Well, it did for some years—until Berwanger's days were over. And then we were over in a great big way and died with one gasp, but we didn't admit it for a few years.

TQ: Is there anything that really irks you about Chicago?

MACLEAN: Offhand, no. I think it's kind of a wonderful city and I think it's beautiful, too. And I think Jessie, my wife, helped me to see that, helped me to enlarge my conception of beauty and to see it as a beautiful city. It's marvelous, that's all. And we'd go down at night to the astronomical place—the Planetarium—and go out there on that point and look back across the harbor, back across to the city. One of the most beautiful sights in the world. And it's more beautiful than ever.

I was coming in from O'Hare field the other day. It was a cold glittering day—brilliant sunlight, but cold, and the skyline showed up miles and miles before you usually could see it. All the bad air was cut away. It was stunning. I'm sure those architects never cared a damned bit about the way they placed one building next to the others. But the thing comes out as a magnificent composition.

And sometimes I'd go up the Calumet River to see a kind of industrial beauty up there—great giant cranes coming down, and giant bridges going up and almost collapsing on top of you. It's marvelous up those rivers. It's another kind of beauty. You have to forget how it smells, but, you know, the Post-Impressionists would have loved it. There's picture after picture of this kind of structural beauty. It's not the Blackfoot River, but it's very beautiful.

TQ: There's a kind of beauty about the work—the human work that's involved in there, too.

MACLEAN: Oh, isn't it? Of course I'm attracted to that. That's one reason why I like logging so much. It's a gigantic thing. But a lot of this big urban work and industry is just as gigantic and fabulous. Fabulous what men can move and do. Every time they dig a goddamned basement over at the University for a new building, I can't keep my eyes off that son of a bitch running the crane. He does things with that crane a woman can't do with a sewing machine, they're so delicate. Great blocks. And this crane comes down and picks up the whole thing, takes it way the hell up in the air, hands it over to some guy up there who does marvelous things with it. All as if it were weightless. Incredible! Workmen in the big city.

TQ: Now you seem to feel very much the city is your home.

MACLEAN: If you are going to make another place a second home you have to work both sides of the street. You have to pick spots that are like your first home to keep you from feeling lonely and not in one piece. That's why I like the Morton Arboretum and Palos Park. I can get in my car at the University and in twenty-five minutes I can be where there are wild deer and beaver. The other side of the street is the Calumet River and the giant cranes and gigantic structural beauty. And the skyline as you look across the harbor at night from the Planetarium—it may be the most beautiful city sight in the world.

Yes, I like this place. I feel—I truly feel, without any schizophrenia any more—I really feel that I am someone with two homes, and they're not very different really. I've been careful to see they didn't get too different.

The Old Man and the River

Pete Dexter*

Early morning, Seeley Lake, Montana. The sun has touched the lake, but the air is dead-still and cooler than the water, and the fog comes off the surface in curtains, hiding some of the Swan Range three miles to the east. And in doing that, it frames the rest. It is the design here, I think, that nothing is taken without compensation, except by men and fires. They leave all the holes.

On the lake a Cutthroat breaks the surface; pieces of it follow him into the air. He breaks it again, falling back. The water mends itself in circles; the circles disappear. You could never say exactly where, but that's how things mend; it's how you get old, too. Not that they are necessarily different things. The place is quiet again. The sun has touched the lake, but the lake still belongs to the night. To the night and to the old man.

He is in the main room of the cabin putting wood on the fire. I hear him humming—a long, flat note, more electric than musical. I think it is a sound he makes without hearing it. He moves from

*"The Old Man and the River" by Pete Dexter is reprinted from *Esquire* 95 (June 1981), pp. 86, 88-89, 91. Copyright © 1981 by Pete Dexter. Reprinted by permission of the author and the publisher.

the fireplace to the kitchen wearing a fishing hat, runs lake water out of the spigot into a dented two-quart pan, puts that on the stove to heat. He starts a pot of coffee, leaves it on a counter, and pushes out the door to urinate in the yard. He and his father built the cabin in 1922 as a retreat from whatever civilization there was in Missoula, and they didn't do it to come down off the mountains and have to look at an indoor toilet.

He comes back in, humming, and surveys the kitchen. He scratches his cheek, remembering where he is. He locates the coffeepot, checks to see what is inside. Part of him is somewhere else. Probably not so much of him that he'd piss in the fireplace and throw the wood out the door, but it isn't impossible.

The guess is that the part of the old man that's not in the kitchen is someplace tangent to August of 1949, Mann Gulch, Montana, where thirteen of sixteen smoke jumpers were killed in the first hours of a wildfire that got into the crowns of the trees there. He is in the last chapter of that story now—the jumpers have become *his* jumpers, he looks at tall trees and imagines fire in their tops, sucking the oxygen out of the air, and feels how helpless a man is in its presence—and while it's still three hours until he sits down and puts himself back in Mann Gulch to confront it, he is headed there already, feeling his way over what has already been done, measuring what is left.

As far as I know, that's the only pleasure there is in writing—until something's finished, anyway. And the old man works carefully and is entitled to his time alone with what he's done. I stay in bed looking out the window, waiting for him to call me for breakfast.

The book was a Christmas present from my brother Tom. I don't usually read Christmas books. He brought it with him from Chicago, catching a ride east through a blizzard with a girlfriend who wasn't his girlfriend anymore. I'd met her even when she was his girlfriend, and I owed him for coming. Christmas Eve, she put him out at Exit 4 of the New Jersey Turnpike.

So I read it, I think in late March 1980. I had just taken the

Christmas tree out anyway, and when I came back into the house it was lying there in a forty-dollar pile of pine needles. *A River Runs Through It*, by Norman Maclean. It was a thin book, two long stories divided by a shorter story, on the back a picture of an old man who obviously takes no prisoners, looking at you as if you'd just invented rock'n'roll.

That night I called Tom. "Holy shit," I said. "Who is this guy?"

"I had him for Shakespeare," he said.

I said, "The fucker *is* Shakespeare."

Don't tell me literary criticism is a dead art. It turned out Maclean wasn't Shakespeare, but then Shakespeare wasn't a forest ranger. Or a fisherman or a logger. He may not even have been a literature teacher at the University of Chicago, but they don't talk about that there.

Maclean was all of those things, and when he retired from the university at seventy, his two children talked him into writing down some of his stories. *A River Runs Through It* was published in 1976, when he was seventy-three, and the first 104 pages of that book— the title story—filled holes inside me that had been so long in the making that I'd stopped noticing they were there.

It is a story about Maclean and his brother, Paul, who was beaten to death with a gun butt in 1938. It is about not understanding what you love, about not being able to help. It is the truest story I ever read; it might be the best written. And to this day it won't leave me alone.

I thought for a while it was the writing that kept bringing it around. That's the way it comes back to me: I hear the sound of the words, then I see them happen. I spent four hours one afternoon picking out three paragraphs to drop into a column I was writing about the book, and in the end they didn't translate, because except for the first sentence—"In our family, there was no clear line between religion and fly-fishing"—there isn't anything in it that doesn't depend on what comes before it for its meaning.

If that sounds more like building a house than like building a story, it's not an accident. Maclean knows what it is to work with his hands, and for him there is as much art in a cabin as there is in a story, as long as it's as well done. And there are all kinds of stories and all kinds of houses, but only the ones you have lived in matter.

At seven-thirty, Norman Maclean brings in coffee and orange juice.

Seeley Lake lies in the valley between two mountain ranges; the Swan to the east, the Mission to the west. The cabin is on the west side of the lake, built of lodgepole pine on land leased from the U. S. Forest Service in one of the best stands of western larch left in the world. Some of the trees are seven hundred years old. A hundred yards south is a public camping area.

On warm weekends during the summer, the camp fills up with "outsiders"—people from places like Helena and Great Falls. Maclean also calls them "the marijuana set." Sometimes they steal his firewood. "They defile this place. They come in on motorcycles, they yell all weekend and Sunday night they'll steal your dog on the way home."

After August, though, they don't come back. The ski boats disappear from the lake, the fish come back to the surface in the morning and at dusk. "The bears and I take over after Labor Day," he says. "Two of them sat right there on the steps last year. I'd come home from fishing or a walk, and they'd be there waiting for me. I'd honk the car horn, wave my hat. . . ." He touches his head, then frowns. "Did you see my hat?"

We are standing outside. I don't see his hat; on the other hand, I don't see bears. It turns out they are hard cases and won't move for hats anyway. "It's no good for anybody when bears lose their natural fear of men," he says. There is a lot of truth in that—it is two days since a couple of college kids were killed by a bear north of here—but there is a scolding in what he says, and I don't think he would say it except for the lost hat.

Out on the lake a boat bangs past, then a line, a skier. The skier falls. Maclean watches the small explosion in the water—a leg, a ski, a life jacket. "Sink," he says.

For six weeks after Labor Day, Norman Maclean has the west side of the lake to himself. It snows for about ten days in early

September, then turns warm. Every morning he writes, from nine or nine thirty to noon. He sits at a small red table in the middle of his living room—the same table where he's just eaten breakfast—and squeezes out three or four hundred words from Mann Gulch, in longhand. Words that will be rewritten three and four times.

He will not work on the porch; there is too much out there to watch, and he will not indulge himself that there are mornings he can't write. He doesn't have the time. "When it's good," he says, "I see my life coming together in paragraphs."

After the writing he takes a bath in the lake. If it's snowing, he gets cold. In the afternoon he walks or fishes, visiting the lakes and rivers and mountains of his stories, crossing tracks half a century old.

In October it snows again, this time with nothing behind it but more snow, and the old man closes up the cabin and drives back to Chicago to wait out Montana's winter.

"Right here, this was the place," he said. We were standing beneath a pine tree, looking a mile across Holland Lake to the place where runoff from one of the Swan Mountains empties into it. A waterfall. "I used to come here with Jessie before I married her, and tell her what a hell of a fellow I was going to turn out to be. I don't know if she believed that bullshit, but she used to get a far-off look in her eyes. . . .

"Her family was Catholic, but they all jumped the fence somewhere along the line. She was from Wolf Creek, population one hundred eleven, and my father married us in Helena. And that woman kept me in place.

"I used to mourn the loss of my youth. I started when I was about twenty, and one day she said, 'I knew you when you were young, Norman, and you were a goddamn mess.'

"Eighteen years before she died they told her it was hopeless. Emphysema. She wouldn't leave the cigarettes alone. The last years, she lived with an oxygen tank, but she never whined, I never heard her cry. She died in December 1968, in Chicago, and I thought I died with her."

It is my second day at Seeley Lake. Norman has shown me the Pyramid Mountain Lumber Company. Now he wants to show me the nurse. "You're going to love her," he says. "A big, tough talker from Butte. She came here because we had no doctor—they're all in the cities doing research, where the money is. So I went over to see what this nurse was like. She was in another room with a patient.

"I sat down outside and the first thing I heard was, 'Open your mouth wider, you sonofabitch, so I can see how big a pill to throw down there.' A great woman. She knows where I fish, what medicine I need; she and Bud know where to find me if I don't come back. We go off boozing a couple of times a summer, go to some fancy restaurant fifty miles away."

That sounds like a good nurse, all right, but somehow by the time we pack the car—a Thermos of ice water, field glasses, six shots of Ancient Age bourbon in a mason jar, and "Did you see my hat?"—we decide to visit Bud's place instead. Bud Moore is his friend who at sixty-three still runs thirty miles of traplines up into the mountains, who walked his wife almost to death taking her into the Idaho wilderness for their honeymoon.

The place is twenty-six miles north on blacktop, another three and a half over gravel. The only way in or out after December is by snowmobile or snowshoes. Maclean uses his little car without lugging the engine; he doesn't have to stop talking to shift. He understands the car, but then, he understands the canned peaches in his refrigerator. He can tell you where in Oregon they come from, how they're canned, and maybe what is done with the pit. He knows his furniture, each of his trees, every log in his cabin— faults and graces—all on a personal basis. He knows everything he touches. Knowing what has touched him has been harder.

"When I tell you how to pack a mule," he says, "goddammit, that's how you pack a mule." He is talking here about his stories, but the stories are as much a part of Maclean as he is of them, and a man like this doesn't start writing at seventy to flirt with the truth, or the language. "I got five hundred letters about the book," he says, "a lot of them from fishermen. There's no bastards in the world who like to argue more than fishermen, and not one of them corrected me on anything. That is my idea of a good review.

"I knew when I started that it was too late for me to be a writer, that all I could hope to do was write a few things well." We are bouncing up Bud Moore's road now. "I assemble pieces of ordinary speech. Every little thing counts. You take the way it comes to you first, with adjectives and adverbs, and cut out all the crap. You use an adjective, it better be a sixty-four-dollar adjective. Turn off the faucet and let them come out one drop at a time."

It took more than two years to put together the 217 pages that make up *A River Runs Through It*. "At the end," he says, "I was almost afraid to sleep, afraid I'd lose the connections as it came together."

When the book was finished, three New York publishers turned it down as "western." One of them wrote to point out, "These stories have trees in them." Finally it was the University of Chicago Press that took the book, the only work of fiction it has ever published.

In 1977 *A River* was nominated by the Pulitzer Prize fiction jury, but the advisory board decided not to make the award, calling it "a lean year for fiction."

I know just enough about the Pulitzer people to guess that what happened was that one of them noticed the trees too. The movie offers came in anyway.

"Now, there," he says, "is a bunch that eats what they find run over on the road. One studio sent out some soft-talker first to tell me about art and the integrity of what I'd written. Then they sent me a yellow-dog contract saying they could do what they wanted with my stories, that they could publish a book about the movie—about my stories, my brother, the people I loved and love—and choose anybody they wanted to write it. I told them, 'When we had bastards like you out West, we shot them for coyote bait.'

"So the studio people turned it over to their New York attorneys—that's as low as it goes, New York lawyers who can't make it in New York and go to California—and they studied the situation for a year and discovered the book was autobiographical. I've got a cardboard box full of letters, and it was eighteen months before anybody read the sonofabitching book.

"Another year passed, and another soft-talker showed up, saying he cared about art. I told him what had happened with the studio, but he was with an independent producer. He said it would be different, and the next thing that came in the mail was the same goddamn yellow-dog contract that no West Virginia coal miner would sign. They said they had to have artistic control. Not with my family, my stories. Nobody else is going to touch them."

I ask if he ever thinks about what he might have written if he'd started earlier. He shakes his head. "I try to live without regrets. Besides, I think there are probably patterns and designs to our lives. Mostly, of course, it's fuck-ups, but there are designs too. . . ."

Norman Maclean didn't go to school until he was ten. The truant officers got him while he was out hunting. His father was an immigrant Scottish Presbyterian minister and had kept his older son at home and educated him himself.

Paul was three years younger and went to school. Mornings the brothers studied, afternoons they went into the woods or fished the Big Blackfoot, a river the family came to look on as its own. The brothers were fighters and fishermen. Paul was a gambler, a drinker, a genius outdoors. He became a reporter for a small newspaper in Helena, and later, when he was killed, it was probably over gambling debts. The men who beat him to death were never caught. Norman was less of a gambler, less of a drinker, less of a genius outdoors, and he went to Dartmouth, where one of his teachers was Robert Frost.

"I don't think Frost ever read a paper any of us wrote," he says. "We'd meet once a week around the fireplace in the basement of the chairman of the English department's house. Frost would just walk back and forth in front of the fireplace and talk and talk and talk. Dramatic monologues. There was a sense of character in everything he said and everything he wrote. I am directly indebted to him. As a writer of prose, my debts are nearly all to poets."

Maclean graduated from Dartmouth and taught there two years.

He came back to Montana and worked for the U. S. Forest Service for another two years. Then he went to the University of Chicago as a graduate assistant, teaching three sessions of English composition.

"The University of Chicago is a tough place. I had to get drunk Friday night so I could spend all weekend in bed, marking papers." And summers he would come home to Montana, trying somehow to marry the things he found beautiful—the woods and the language—and live with them both. He would do that all his life, but his talent was teaching.

"It's like shooting a scatter-gun, or fishing, or anything else," Maclean says. "Take a collie out into the field every day of his life, show him a bird and hold his tail straight, he isn't going to learn to point. And if you don't have the genes, you can teach until you die and never be better than a C- or a D + ..."

Three times Maclean was given the University of Chicago's award for excellence in undergraduate teaching—an award that traditionally is given only once. There have been honorary degrees from other universities; the last one, from Montana State University at Bozeman, particularly touched him. He is professor emeritus at Chicago, and there is a scholarship in his name, set up by some of his former students. One of those students is Supreme Court Justice John Paul Stevens, who from time to time tells a law-school class that the best way he knows to prepare for the law is to take Shakespeare from Norman Maclean.

"Shakespeare," Maclean says—"he must have known more about writing than anybody else ever did. Every year I said to myself, 'You better teach this bastard so you don't forget what great writing is like.' I taught him technically, two whole weeks for the first scene from *Hamlet*. I'd spend the first day on just the first line, 'Who's there?' "

Bud Moore's house sits on high ground between two ponds, a two-story log cabin he built himself. From the corner of the porch you can see the Swan Mountains; turning your head, you see the Missions. "Look at the notch work," Maclean says. "Look at the selection of logs. People think log cabins are a lost art, but the truth is they're better now. The old ones were generally built with the same trees they cleared to build on. You could stand in the middle of the living room and the wind would blow your hat off. . . ."

While he looks for his hat, I read a note on the front door. Bud is in the Bob Marshall Wilderness on the other side of the Swans. He went in with his dogs and his grandson a day or two ago and is not expected back for a week.

"There is a lake on the other side," he said. We were a mile from the base of one of the Swan Mountains. "Paul and I would climb over in the morning, catch our limit in George Lake, and climb back at night."

He studied the mountain. A steep, hard climb. Two thirds of the way up, the trees stop growing. "Goddamn, I wish I were good enough to do that again." The name of a lady we both know somehow got into it then. "Of course I would follow her up there," he said. "Who would mind breaking a leg like that?"

Maclean walks over to the tent where Bud Moore lived during the two years he was building the cabin. He shows me where a grizzly was shot trying to get in. "That bear ran half a mile after the bullet passed through his heart," he says. "After he was dead, that's how much hate he had, a half mile. . . . You can feel that sometimes in a Rainbow too. . . ."

He heads downhill through some woods, tripping now and then on fallen trees. He doesn't slow down. "Being old isn't great," he says, "but you can't kick when most of your colleagues are on the other side of the ground."

On the way down he identifies trees by which needles are best to sleep on: Balsam fir is good. Spruce, you might as well sleep standing up. He points out the different wild flowers. "There's Indian paintbrush . . . there's fireweed . . . there's bear shit, over near that aspen tree. . . ."

Bear shit strikes me as a colorful western name for a wild flower: I can picture little bunches of it growing here and there up to a tree with a beehive. But it turns out bear shit is bear shit, even in Montana. I ask, "I don't suppose you can tell which way the bear was going?" but the old man is already moving ahead, humming. We come to a clearing, the site of a small abandoned sawmill. It is where the grizzly ran out of hate. We stand there a moment admiring the spot.

On the way back we stop at a fork of the Swan River, which is the river he fishes when he isn't fishing the Blackfoot. It is more peaceful than the Blackfoot and runs in sight of mountain peaks where there is always snow.

The Blackfoot is wider and faster and unforgiving, its view is largely a canyon, and the fish he catches there, sometimes he can feel them hate. The Blackfoot is where he crosses time. It was the Swan, though, where Bud Moore found him last summer. Lying out on some rocks, not knowing what had happened to him.

Back at the cabin we sit together on a log near the porch and drink bourbon and ice water out of the Thermos cap. I ask about it. "I don't know what happened," he says. "I was fishing, I must have slipped." He isn't asking for help.

I hand him the Thermos lid; we drink liquor and look at Bud Moore's place. He smiles at the electrical wires leading in. "She'll have him putting in a toilet next," he says.

From the log I can see the tops of the Mission Range. The old man has been there and left his tracks in everlasting snow. It is coming together now, mending, he sees it in paragraphs, is almost afraid to sleep for losing the connections.

He asks for no help.

He knows that when the time comes there are friends who will know where to look. "Come back," he says. "We'll go fishing."

When I look over, his eyes are in the branches of Bud Moore's tallest trees, imagining a fire in the crowns. He begins to hum.

Studio portrait of Norman Fitzroy Maclean at 2 years and 9 months.

Norman Maclean's father, John Norman Maclean. No date. Photo by Norman Maclean.

Above left: *Norman Maclean's mother, Clara Davidson Maclean, at the kitchen window of the family cabin at Seeley Lake, Montana, September 20, 1933. Photo by Norman Maclean.*

Below left: *Jessie Burns Maclean; her mother, Florence Burns; her brother, Art Burns; and children Jean and John Maclean: 1947. Photo taken at Seeley Lake, Montana, behind the cabin Norman and his father built in 1922. Photo by Norman Maclean.*

Jessie Burns. Engagement photograph taken sometime between 1929 and 1930.

Studio portrait of Paul Maclean. No date.

Above: *Norman Maclean,*
Instructor at The University of
Chicago, circa 1931.

Norman Maclean's brother, Paul,
probably taken the year before his
murder in Chicago in 1938. Photo
by Norman Maclean.

Norman Maclean. English 237: Shakespeare. January 22, 1970.
Photos by Leslie Strauss.

Left: *Norman Maclean and Laird Robinson in 1981, the year Norman received his honorary degree from the University of Montana.*

Below: *Editor Hugh Nichols with Norman Maclean in Goat Canyon on the Lochsa River. May, 1987. Photo by Robert Wrigley*

Essays
in Appreciation
and Criticism

Haunted by Waters

Wallace Stegner*

The writing career of Norman Maclean is a phenomenon.
A retired English professor from the University of Chicago at the
age of seventy begins, secretly and almost shamefacedly, to write
down the stories of his youth that he has told his children. He pro-
duces three stories of such unfashionable length and kind—among
other defects, "they have trees in them"—that no magazine or trade
publisher is interested. Through the influence of friends, they are
finally brought out by the University of Chicago Press, which never
published any fiction before that and so far as I know has published
none since.

This slim book, virtually without reviews or advertising, finds its
way into hands that pass it on to other hands. Fly fishermen discover it first, with delight, but others besides fishermen respond to
it. A little group of admirers forms and spreads. A second printing
is needed, then a third, then a paperback edition. By word of mouth
a reputation is born. Now, ten years after his first and only fictions
saw print, this author of three stories is an established name, an

*This essay was written especially for this volume and appears here for the first time
with the permission of the author.

authentic western voice, respected and imitated, and books are being written about him.

Why? How? Every writer and publisher wishes he knew. The usual channels of publicity and criticism had virtually nothing to do with it. Neither did literary fashion, for that, along with the orthodoxies of contemporary short story form, is simply ignored in these stories.

For one thing, they are "realistic," and realism, as everyone knows, was long since left to the second-raters. For another, they are about the West, an environment of broad hats and low foreheads, a place traditionally short of thought and with only rudimentary feelings. For still another, they are about a *historical* West, Montana in the years during and just after World War I, a West that was less a society than a passing phase of the frontier; and they contain some of the mythic feeling and machinery, the crudeness, the colorful characters, and the ox-stunning fist fights made all too familiar by horse opera.

Don't look here for the economy and precision that have marked the short story at least since Joyce and in some ways since Poe. The characteristic modern short story starts as close to its end as it can. It limits itself to a unified action, often a single scene, and to the characters absolutely essential to that action. It covers the time and space required, no more, and picks up the past, insofar as it needs it, in passing. Ibsen perfected that "uncovering" technique in his plays a hundred years ago, rediscovering for both drama and fiction Aristotle's three unities.

But two of Maclean's stories spread across whole summers, and the third contains an entire life. In all three the action moves around—mountains to town, town to the Big Blackfoot to Wolf Creek, camp to cafe, cafe to bar. Instead of a rigidly limited cast of characters, whole communities inhabit these tales: rangers, cooks, dynamiters, packers, pimps, whores, waitresses with and without freckles, bartenders, barflies, family, in-laws, small-town doctors, horses, and coyote-killing dogs. Around their discursive actions a world grows up. Inclusion, not exclusion, is the intention; amplitude, not economy, is the means.

Furthermore, this writer talks to his readers, guesses at the motivations of characters, sums up, drops one-liners of concentrated observation and wisdom. He is garrulous and personal. The puppeteer shows his hands and feet. No wonder he couldn't find an orthodox publisher.

It is instructive to note what is not here, but more so to note what is. All three of these stories, even "Logging and Pimping," the first-written, shortest, and least-satisfying, grow on re-reading. The two longer ones grow a great deal. Things missed or only half seen edge out into the open. Things that looked only reported turn out to have been *rendered*. Throwaway lines reveal unexpected pertinence, discursiveness that we first forgave as naivete has to be reappraised as deep cunning. Maybe Maclean knew fully what he was doing, maybe he only moved by instinct sharpened through years of studying literature, maybe his hand was guided by love and nostalgia for places and people long left behind. However he did it, he made a world.

The Montana of his youth was a world with the dew on it. Perhaps the time of youth always has dew on it, and perhaps that is why we respond to Maclean's evocation of his. But I lived in Montana, or close to it, during those same years, and it was a world younger, fresher, and more touched with wonder and possibility than any I have since known. After seventy years, I still dream it; and when it is revived by these stories it glows with a magical light, like one of those Ansel Adams photographs that are more magnificent than the scenes they pretend to represent.

The remembered and evoked world of barely-touched wilderness and barely-formed towns has, for all its primitiveness, violence, and freedom, an oddly traditional foundation. A raw society, it offers to growing boys mainly a set of physical skills—riding, shooting, fishing, packing, logging, fire-fighting, fist-fighting—and a code to go with them. The hero, the admired and imitated person, is one who does something superlatively well. To fail at a skill, if you try your best, is unfortunate but respectable; to fail in nerve or trying is to merit contempt.

It is absolutely right that the seventeen-year-old Norman Maclean of "USFS 1919" should model himself on Bill Bell, the best ranger, best packer, best all-around mountain man, and best fighter in the Bitterroot country. It is right that in "Logging and Pimping" a grown-up Norman Maclean should half kill himself keeping up with the sadistic logger-pimp Jim. It is right that in "A River Runs Through It" he and his brother, trained by their father in fly fishing and its mysteries, should reserve their deepest contempt for bait fishermen. Skill is both competitive and proud. As the basis of a code, it can be harshly coercive on attitudes and conduct.

Also, it is not enough. Unaccompanied by other more humane qualities, skill can produce a bully like Jim or a tinhorn like the cook. The code goes beyond skill to character; for those who subscribe to it, it defines a man. A man for young Norman Maclean is neither mouthy nor finicky; he is stoical in the face of pain; he does not start fights but he tries to finish them; he does what his job and his morality tell him to do. But he cannot get by on mere skill. He needs something else, some decency or compassion that can only be learned from such sources as the boys' preacher father. In the beginning, he reminds his son, was the Word.

I knew a few P.K.'s in my youth. Most were Scottish. All had to learn to reconcile the harsh, limited, demanding code of their frontier society with the larger codes in which grace and personal salvation ultimately lie. Norman Maclean learned that. His brother Paul, with more skills, with every advantage except the capacity to transcend the code of his place and time, did not.

I speak as if the stories were about real people. I think they are. Maclean gives us no reason to make a distinction between real and fictional people. The stories are so frankly autobiographical that one suspects he hasn't even bothered to alter names. The only thing that has happened to young Maclean's experience is that it has been recollected in tranquillity, seen in perspective, understood, and fully felt. The stories are a distillation, almost an exorcism.

The Maclean boys grew up in a world "overbearing with challenges" and dominated by the code. Sent to the fire-watch station on Grave Peak, sure that he has been sent off as punishment for his dislike of the cook, young Maclean responds by trying to do the job so well, in spite of rattlers, grizzlies, and lightning storms, that Bell will have to admit he has been unjust. (Bell doesn't; he takes the performance for granted.) Pulling all day on the end of a seven-foot crosscut whose other end is in the hands of a bully determined to put him down, Maclean would die on the saw rather than admit he was even tired. Told to go for the money if a fight breaks out, he goes for it, though he knows he will get his face busted. Commanded to take his impossible brother-in-law fishing, he and Paul do, though they would rather drown him.

In every case the reward for faithfulness is acceptance. The logger-pimp Jim learns enough respect for Maclean to make him a "pal." Bill Bell, making up for the whole unsatisfactory summer, asks him to join the crew again next year. And the women caretakers of the impossible brother-in-law let him know without saying it (they are no more mouthy than their men) that he has done his duty, that the failure is not his.

These rites of passage through observance of the code, these steps toward a simplistically-understood manhood, dominate both "Logging and Pimping" and "USFS 1919," and are present in "A River Runs Through It." But they are not enough to account for the astonishing success of Maclean's little book. The fact is, the title story contains everything that the other two do, and far surpasses them, transcends them. It flies where they walk. Where they are authentic, humorous, ironic, observant, and much else, "A River Runs Through It" is both poetic and profound.

In the other stories the skills under discussion are work skills from a half-forgotten time. They are recreated as lovingly as Melville recreates the boats, the gear, the try-works, and the rest of his cetology. They pack the crevices of the narrative with a dense exposition of *process*. Getting up from reading, we could make a pass at fighting a forest fire or balancing the load on a mule.

But fishing with a dry fly, which is the skill that gives both meaning and form to "A River Runs Through It," is not labor but an art, not an occupation but a passion, not a mere skill but a mystery, a symbolic reflection of life.

Fly fishing renounces the pragmatic worms and hardware of the meat fishermen. It is truly an art, "an art that is performed on a four-count rhythm between ten and two o'clock." It calls for coordination, control, and restraint more than for strength. To do it right you need not only skill but the imagination to think like a fish. It has its rituals and taboos, and thus is an index to character like the code, but far subtler. There is no clear distinction between it and religion. It takes place in wild natural places, which for Maclean mean awe, holiness, respect; and in water, which he feels as the flow of time.

Like the lesser skills, fly fishing has its arrogance. Witness Paul's response to Izaak Walton's *Compleat Angler*: not only is Walton a bait fisherman but the sonofabitch can't even spell "complete." The pride of a supreme artist, plus an unswerving adherence to the code, is a recipe for disaster, a fatal flaw. Despite his artistry and his grace, Paul is one who cannot be helped because he will not accept help. Some saving intelligence, a capacity to see beyond or around the code, saves Paul's brother, but his brother cannot save Paul.

So is this a story of *hubris* in the Bitterroots, of a young god destroyed by pride? If it is, why all that other stuff the story contains— all that tawdry story of looking after the incompetent, mouthy brother-in-law, all that bawdy farce of the whore Old Rawhide and the sunburned backsides? If this is a story of pathetic or tragic failure, why is it cluttered up with so much exposition of the art of fishing, so many stories of fishing expeditions, so many homilies from the preacher father, so many hints about the relations of Norman Maclean with his wife's family? An impressive story as it stands, would this be even more impressive if it were cleaned up, straightened up, and tucked in?

I will tell you what I think. I only think it, I don't know it; but once when I suggested it in Norman Maclean's presence he didn't deny it. Perhaps, like Robert Frost, he thinks a writer is entitled to anything a reader can find in him. Perhaps I persuaded him of something he hadn't realized. More likely, he knew it all along.

The fact is, or I think it is, that this apparently rambling yarn is made with the same skill that Paul displays while fishing the Big

Blackfoot, the same deliberation and careful refusal to hurry, the same reading of the water. "It is not fly fishing if you are not looking for the answers to questions," the author says, and this is big water demanding every skill.

Listen to how Paul fishes—(this is early in the story, and may be taken as a forecast of what is to come):

> The river above and below his rock was all big Rainbow water, and he would cast hard and low upstream, skimming the water with his fly but never letting it touch. Then he would pivot, reverse his line in a great oval above his head, and drive his line low and hard downstream, again skimming the water with his fly. He would complete this grand circle four or five times, creating an immensity of motion which culminated in nothing if you did not know, even if you could not see, that now somewhere out there a small fly was washing itself on a wave. Shockingly, immensity would return as the Big Blackfoot and the air above it became iridescent with the arched sides of a great Rainbow.
>
> He called this "shadow casting," and frankly I don't know whether to believe the theory behind it—that the fish are alerted by the shadows of flies passing over the water by the first casts, so hit the fly the moment it touches the water. It is more or less the "working up an appetite" theory, almost too fancy to be true, but then every fine fishermen has a few fancy stunts that work for him and for almost no one else. Shadow casting never worked for me. . . .

But if shadow casting never worked for the fisherman Norman Maclean, it works marvelously well for the fictionist. He fills the air with flies that never really settle, he dazzles us with loops of glittering line, he keeps us watching Old Rawhide, who does not matter at all, and the brother-in-law, who matters only in that he demonstrates the lack of everything that makes Paul special, and he keeps us from watching Paul, who does matter. Then, on page 102 of a 104-page story, the fly settles, and we strike at what we have been alerted to but have not been allowed to anticipate.

Bluntly, brutally, in a few hundred words, the important part of the story is ended with Paul's life; the shadow falls suddenly on a tale that has been often sunny, even farcical. Time comes down like a curtain, what has been vibrantly alive is only remembered, we are left hollow with loss, and we end in meditation on the Big Black-foot in the cool of the evening, in the Arctic half-light of the canyon, haunted by waters.

The ending is brought off with such economy only because it was earlier obscured by all the shadow casting. A real artist has been fishing our stream, and the art of fishing has been not only his message but his form and his solace. An organ should be playing Bach's *Es Ist Vollbracht*.

"A River Runs Through It" is a story rooted in actuality, in known people and remembered events. But it is a long way from a limited realism. It is full of love and wonder and loss, it has the same alternations of sunshine and shadow that a mountain stream has, and its meaning can be heard a long way from its banks. It is an invitation to memory and the pondering of our lives. "To me," Maclean remarks in his introduction, "the constant wonder has been how strange reality has been."

Fisherman or not, who is not haunted by waters?

Norman Maclean's
Two-Hearted River

Harold P. Simonson*

"In our family, there was no clear line between religion and fly fishing" (1). With this arresting opener, Norman Maclean begins his novella, "A River Runs Through It" (1976), the first work of original fiction ever published by the University of Chicago Press in its long history. It is also Maclean's own first work of fiction, written after his return to Montana following retirement as William Rainey Harper Professor of English at the University of Chicago. Remarkable in many ways, his novella deserves recognition as (I believe) a classic in western American literature. As for the analogy between religion and fly fishing, Maclean hooks it, plays and fights it, and finally lands it with masterful form. In short, the analogy works artistically. Moreover, the river (Montana's Big Blackfoot River) takes on intriguing dimensions, which I will argue include both symbolic and typological significance. For the author, his closing sentence says it all: "I am haunted by waters" (104).

Christ's disciples were fishermen, those on the Sea of Galilee were

*"Norman Maclean's Two-Hearted River" by Harold P. Simonson is reprinted from *Western American Literature* 17 (August 1982), pp. 149-155. Copyright © 1982 by Harold P. Simonson. Reprinted by permission of the author and the publisher.

fly fishermen, and Maclean's favorite, John, had to be a *dry-fly* fisherman. This was the logic Maclean as a boy learned from his father's Presbyterian sermons. Yet for all the sermons preached and heard, and all the hours the boy and his brother Paul studied *The Westminster Shorter Catechism*, what really restored their souls, including that of their clergyman father, was to be in the western Montana hills where trout rivers run deep and fast. Ernest Hemingway had said in "Big Two-Hearted River" that swamp fishing was a "tragic adventure"; for Maclean, fishing the Big Blackfoot River was a redemptive one, thanks not only to divine grace but to self-discipline. The theology is sound Calvinism: God does all, man does all.

As for human nature, theologically speaking, just try to use a fly rod for the first time and, says the author, "you will soon find it factually and theologically true that man by nature is a damned mess" (3). Again, Calvin couldn't have said it better. Only the "redeemed" know how to use it. Until such time, a person "will always take a fly rod too far back, just as natural man always overswings with an ax or golf club and loses all his power somewhere in the air" (3). Natural man does everything wrong; he has fallen from an original state of harmony. And he will continue to be a mess until through grace and discipline he learns to cast "Presbyterian-style" (3). The great lesson the father taught his two sons was that "all good things—trout as well as eternal salvation—come by grace and grace comes by art and art does not come easy" (4).

All this theological business isn't as heavy-handed as it sounds. Indeed, Maclean transforms it into characterization, metaphor, humor, and fine detail. He also transforms memories of his father and brother into Rembrandt portraiture edged in darkness and tragedy but also pervaded by a haunting presence, a prelapsarian truth associated with sacred origins, the divine *logos*. Maclean would have us see fishing as a rite, an entry into "oceanic" meanings and eternities compressed into moments, epiphanous "spots of time," the *mysterium tremendum*. Entering the river to fish its dangerous waters is to fish eternity, and to unite in love with those few persons who also obey the exacting code. No one obeyed the code more religiously than brother Paul who, when entering the river, made fishing into a world perfect and apart, a place where joy comes first in a perfect cast, then in a strike that makes the magic "wand" jump convulsively, and finally in a big rainbow trout in the basket—in all, a performance of mastery and art.

Narrator Maclean remembers his brother Paul as a master dry-fly fisherman, indeed as a true artist when holding a four-and-a-half ounce rod in his hand. But more, Paul was one for whom the river in its sacrality held answers to questions, and for whom fly fishing was the search for those answers. That, Paul said, was what fly fishing was, and "you can't catch fish if you don't dare go where they are" (42). Paul dared, and he showed his brother and his Presbyterian father, both expert fishermen too, how to dare. On what was to be their last fishing trip together, before Paul's murder and the father's later death, all things seemed to come together—the river, the fishing, the father and two sons. Sinewing the union was love, and in the union the powerful Big Blackfoot River spoke to them.

It is truly a redemptive moment, caught and held secure in Maclean's memory and in his narrative art. I find it difficult to restrain my admiration; I find Maclean in this story equal to anything in Hemingway and a good deal more courageous, theologically.

In order for this assertion to sink in, I need to emphasize that Maclean's theology includes a doctrine of man. To reiterate, Maclean says that man is a "damned mess." Maclean's courage comes not in asserting this doctrine, which Hemingway and numberless other twentieth-century writers have had no trouble with, but in juxtaposing it with a doctrine of salvation. Without the juxtaposition, damnation is no less a bromide than is salvation. The courage comes in one's affirming a larger context of reality in which the juxtaposition both is and is not reconciled. To change the image, we might imagine a world where a river runs *through* it but is not *of* it. The test of courage is to embrace the paradox.

As for the messiness unto damnation, Maclean's story does not equivocate. The world is a fallen one, people are liars and cheats, family entanglements ruin the most blessed vision. When the narrator's brother-in-law steps off the train at Wolf Creek, we see in

Neal the genus, *phonus bolonus,* dressed in white flannels, a red-and-white-and-blue V-neck sweater over a red-and-white-and-blue turtleneck sweater, and elegant black-and-white shoes. At Black Jack's Bar his big talk with oldtimers and the town's whore, Old Rawhide, shows him in his true element. The family picnic the following day on the Elkhorn River shows him disgustingly out of it. He fishes not with flies but worms and gets nothing; he whimpers from his hangover and feigns sickness to avoid picnic chores. A genuine bastard, he doesn't deserve the solicitude he gets, and he wouldn't get it except for family loyalty. The two brothers know he doesn't even deserve Montana. Neil violates everything that is good, including the code of fishing. On a subsequent trip he violates a trust by stealing beer that the two brothers have left to cool in the river—and in *this,* the Big Blackfoot River. Even worse, he has brought not only a coffee can of worms for bait but also Old Rawhide, and has screwed his whore on a sand bar in the middle of "our family river." The brothers find the two asleep, naked and sunburned. On the cheeks of her ass they see the tattooed letters: LO / VE. The river sanctuary has been defiled; never again will the brothers throw a line here at this hole.

Close as narrator Maclean appears to be to his brother Paul, both reverencing the river whose secrets only the best dry-fly fisherman can hope to touch, a vast gulf nevertheless separates them. If they both find the river an oceanic enigma where answers lie hidden in watery shadows, the narrator finds his brother an enigma as well.

That Paul seeks answers in fishing leaves his brother wondering about the questions being asked. Somewhere deep in Paul's shadowy inner world is chaos that the four-count rhythm of casting has not disciplined, a hell that grace has not transformed. Yet Paul seeks no help either from brother or father. Only the visible things show— namely, that he drinks and gambles and fights too much, that gambling debts translate into enemies, that his job as reporter on a Helena newspaper confirms a world full of bastards, and, finally, that he wants no help, asks for none, expects none except what the hard-driving river can bring. Clearly, Paul lives in a world more profoundly fallen than that represented even by Neal's damned messiness. Confirmation of this fact comes in the manner of Paul's death: beaten by the butt of a revolver, nearly all the bones of his right hand (his fighting hand) broken, and his body dumped in an alley—this, the death of a dry-fly fisherman whose rod was a wand of magical power and beauty, and who, when inhabiting this river-world, embodied laughter and discipline and joy.

Wherein, then, is saving grace? In the water? In the words that the father reads in his Greek New Testament? In the Word, the *logos,* from the Fourth Gospel that the father seeks to interpret as the two of them, father and son, wait on the riverbank to watch Paul catch his final big fish? ''In the part I was reading,'' the father explains, ''it says the Word was in the beginning, and that's right. I used to think water was first, but if you listen carefully you will hear that the words are underneath the water'' (95).

Now comes the crucial distinction.

''If you ask Paul,'' the son says, ''he will tell you that the words are formed out of water'' (96).

''No,'' the father replies, ''you are not listening carefully. The water runs over the words. Paul will tell you the same thing'' (96).

Of course, Paul never tells, and we suspect he never found out. Neither his brother nor his father knows the truth about him. Yet the distinction deserves close attention together with the images that Maclean allows to arise from his memory, images that come out of the past to bear new meanings, joining the past and the present in the image and the image bearing the truth.

Watery images bring forth fish seen sometimes as ''oceanic,'' with their black spots resembling crustaceans. The river itself flows from origins shaped by the ice age, the rocks by more elemental forces emanating ''almost from the basement of the world and time'' (84). The rain is the same as ''the ancient rain spattering on mud before it became rock . . . nearly a billion years ago'' (84). Whereas in the sunny world where the river-voice is ''like a chatterbox, doing its best to be friendly,'' in the dark shadows where the river ''was deep and engaged in profundities'' and where it circled back on itself now and then ''to say things over to be sure it had understood itself''—in these primal depths the voice issues from a ''subterranean river'' where only the most courageous ever venture and where only *real* fishing takes place (95).

Through such imagery Maclean takes us to foundations antecedent to water. From these foundations the father in the narrative hears words—words beneath the water, words before the water. The distinction between words formed out of water and words formed out of foundations beneath the water is the distinction between mystical pantheism and the Christian *logos.* The distinction is between the *unity* of creator and creation on the one hand and their *separation* on the other. Again, the distinction is between the saving grace found in one's merging with nature, and that found in one's belonging to the God antecedent to nature, the God in nature but not of nature, immanent yet transcendent. And whatever the word spoken in the pantheistic unity, it is not the same as that spoken in the separateness, spoken in the *logos,* spoken from under and before the timeless rocks.

I am not suggesting that Maclean, the author, is involved in mere theological dialectic. What he is saying is not what comes from such abstractions but from memory and images, from time past when he and his father and brother were one in love if not in understanding. And now those he loved but did not understand are dead. ''But,'' he adds, ''I still reach out to them'' (104). Something of this love he still hears in the waters of the river and in the foundations beneath. Perhaps he hears the Word itself as did John of the Fourth Gospel. This is what the father must have heard too and what his brother Paul did not. Whether the words come from water or from the deeper foundations, they are words his memory translates into those of father and brother, words that spoke of love. In their words he has his epiphany, yes his redemption, and thus he can say, ''I am haunted by waters.''

I said earlier that Maclean's story is a classic, deserving a place in the pantheon of western American literature. Putting aside such matters as structure and tone, characterization, imagery, and a hundred other elements that subtly harmonize (whether the art be that of Maclean's fiction or his fishing), I find something else, something identifying the river as *symbol* and *type*.

As for symbol, all the age-old meanings associated with living waters—one immediately thinks of purification, fertility, and renewed life—are predicated upon a perceiving mind and a symbolic mode of perception. I'm concerned here more with the act of perception than with the object, more with the perceiver than the perceived or percept. In short, the perceiver as symbolist finds significance through the interaction of experience and imagination, whereas the perceiver as typologist finds significance through a sacred design that is prior to, and independent of, the self. The mode of perception makes all the difference, and in this analysis the two modes are radically different. Symbolism eventuates in a direct interpretation of life, whereas typology relates to history, prophecy, teleology. The symbol is created in the womb of the perceiver's imagination, whereas the type is revealed within the perceiver's faith. Again, the symbolist possesses a special quality enabling him to fuse object and meaning; the typologist possesses a special but different quality enabling him to see what has already been fused and now revealed but is separate from, and independent of, him. Finally, the symbolist enters the river, as it were, and is redeemed by the waters which his imagination transforms into purification and renewal. But the typologist enters what has already been transformed or, more accurately, what flows from a sacred design, purpose, or destiny, made visible through the regenerate eyes and ears of faith.

In Maclean's story the two modes of perception show the river as both symbol and type. When attention is upon Paul's marvelous artistry, validating the halo of spray often enclosing him, we see by means of the narrator's imagination not only a transformed fisherman but a river metamorphosed into a world apart. Fishing becomes a world apart, a world perfect, an imagined and sinless world fusing person with vision. For Paul, when he steadied himself and began to cast, "the whole world turned to water" (20). The narrator shares in the imagined oneness of his brother's world.

But the narrator does not lose himself in it. He also hears his father's words bespeaking a separate design, revealed as the logos or Word that was in the beginning—before the river and before human imaginings. More than speech, this Word is divine action, creating, revealing, redeeming. That the father carries his Greek New Testament along with his fishing rod is a fact not lost upon the author as narrator. Through his father's faith the son reaches out to hear this other Word. No wonder he is haunted by waters.

In truth, the river runs through his mind and consciousness and language and life. But something also runs through the river itself, something that is in it but not of it, something more elemental than water.

WORKS CITED

Maclean, Norman. *A River Runs Through It and Other Stories*. Chicago: University of Chicago Press, 1976.

Fishing for the Words of Life: Norman Maclean's "A River Runs Through It"

"In our family," writes Norman Maclean, "there was no clear line between religion and fly fishing" (1). In "A River Runs Through It," he is faithful to family tradition. As he pays tribute to the art of fishing, especially as practiced by his younger brother Paul, he fishes with words for the words of life that his father, a Presbyterian minister, heard beneath the river's current. In so doing, Maclean is also faithful to the tradition of piscatory prose as established by Izaak Walton's *The Compleat Angler*. It is a generous prose, one that reflects and fosters a love for its subject, one that will not be hurried as it circles toward the synthesis of contemplation and action, piety and practice, and beauty and power which, both Maclean and Walton suggest, is the hallmark of genuine art and genuine religion.

This is not to say that "A River Runs Through It" strives to imitate *The Compleat Angler* in either stance or substance. Indeed, Maclean's father warned his teen-age sons against its influence:

*"Fishing for the Words of Life: Norman Maclean's 'A River Runs Through It' " by Walter Hesford is reprinted from *Rocky Mountain Review of Language and Literature* 34 (Winter 1980): 33–45. Reprinted with the permission of the author and the publisher.

"Izaak Walton is not a respectable writer. He was an Episcopalian and a bait fisherman" (5). One suspects or hopes that this was intended to be humorous, though bait fishermen are consistently castigated in the story as unredeemably fallen mortals. Perhaps a more devastating criticism of Walton came from brother Paul, age thirteen or fourteen: "The bastard doesn't even know how to spell 'complete.' Besides, he has songs to sing to dairymaids." Norman, the future professor of English and writer, defends Walton: "Some of those songs are pretty good." Paul, unimpressed, asks, "Whoever saw a dairymaid on the Big Blackfoot River?" (5).

Clearly, western Montana, where the Big Blackfoot runs and where the Macleans grew up, sponsors a different aesthetic from Walton's seventeenth-century English countryside (though this countryside was torn by civil war, and not likely to give unmediated birth to piscatory pastorals). "A River Runs Through It" does not shy away from the rough realities that encompass the author and eventually overcome his brother. As "preacher's kids," they seemed to find it necessary to play rough, to adopt a tough, irreverent stance in order to achieve independent status, a stance still evident in the style of the mature author, but tempered with wit, generosity, and wisdom. Maclean's witty assertion that his father "told us about Christ's disciples being fishermen, and we were left to assume, as my brother and I did, that all first-class fishermen on the Sea of Galilee were fly fishermen and that John, the favorite, was a dry-fly fisherman" (1) would certainly have shocked Walton, who took devout pride in his holy precursors (46). The reader, however, should not be misled into taking lightly Maclean's discipleship. His irreverence ultimately does reverence to his brother, whose keeper he proves, and keeps alive the faith of his father. He is thus truly pious, and as seriously committed as Walton was to exploring the religious significance of his subject.

*   *   *

Maclean's efforts, I think, may most fruitfully be compared with those of Henry David Thoreau. Thoreau's first book, *A Week on the Concord and Merrimack Rivers*, is replete with a Waltonian catalogue of fish that inhabit Concord waters, and with portraits of anglers who inhabit Concord, the most complete of whom, fittingly, is an Englishman by birth (21–37). In *Walden*, Thoreau portrays himself as a complete angler who, obeying higher laws and an ascetic sensibility, finally transcends the practice altogether (213–214).

There are three strains in Thoreau's piscatory prose that also achieve significance in "A River Runs Through It." The first is an antinomian strain. I am taking the liberties with this old heresy-tainted term usually taken by Americanists, and applying it to the celebration of the truth of the individual heart or consciousness as opposed to the laws of an established religion or society, to the cultivation of inner laws which may supplant the laws of the land. It comes as some surprise that there is even a hint of antinomianism in Walton, the conservative Anglican—though perhaps it shouldn't, when we remember that in his day the Puritans were establishing the law. Walton's true anglers love to be quiet and stay clear of noisy legal affairs (154). They also follow in the footsteps of the holy fishermen who preached *"freedom from the incumbrances of the Law, and a new way to everlasting life"* (46—emphasis Walton), who preached a gospel of religious and social deliverance. It may seem paradoxical that Walton schools his disciples in the tradition and discipline of his art, and at the same time suggests that their traditional predecessors spread freedom. The paradox may be resolved if one believes that the gospel liberates as it fulfills rather than violates the law, that freedom is discipline transfigured. This seems to be the unheretical belief of true anglers, including Thoreau and Maclean.

Thoreau compares with pleasure the free, natural life of the fisherman with the cramped "civil politic life" of a judge; the former, though, perhaps, a social outcast, is wiser, Thoreau implies, than the arbiter of social justice (*A Week*, 21–22). The fishermen Thoreau honors are "wild men, who instinctively follow other fashions and trust other authorities than their townsmen . . ." (*Walden*, 283). What authorities these wild men follow is not clear, but no doubt they are more conducive to their discipline and freedom than are the laws of the land—especially such as might attempt to regulate where and how they should conduct their business. Thoreau spoofs distant legislators who "regulate the number of hooks to be used" at Walden Pond, but "know nothing about the hook of hooks with which to angle for the pond itself, impaling the legislature for bait" (213). Thoreau, one gathers, does know about such a hook. It is his art, with which he has caught forever Walden, and through which he has put to death the old law, establishing for himself and his readers a new law and gospel.

We might expect a romantic like Thoreau to be an antinomian, but we expect to find a taint of the heresy even less in a Presbyterian than in an Anglican. Yet when he gave his sons catechism lessons Sunday afternoons as prelude to a walk on the hills, the Rev. Maclean tried to arouse their hearts rather than their fears: "he never asked us more than the first question in the catechism, 'What is the chief end of man?' And we answered together so one of us could carry on if the other forgot, 'Man's chief end is to glorify God, and to enjoy him forever.' This always seemed to satisfy him, as indeed such a beautiful answer should have, and besides he was anxious to be on the hills where he could restore his soul and be filled to overflowing for the evening sermon" (1).

Though he enjoyed himself in nature, the Rev. Maclean did not believe that man could *naturally* achieve his chief end, either in religion or fly fishing. He held the orthodox position "that man by nature was a mess and had fallen from an original state of grace" (2), a state not easily regained: "all good things," he felt, "—trout as well as eternal salvation—come by grace and grace comes by art and art does not come easy" (4). Art meant "picking up God's rhythms" (for the fly fisherman, this was a "four-count rhythm between ten and two o'clock"). These rhythms enabled man "to regain power and beauty" (2). The poor sinner and poor fisherman were likely "to attain power without recovering grace" (3), and their performance was thus, according to the minister, lacking in the beautiful. "Unlike many Presbyterians," reports his son, "he often used the word 'beautiful' " (2).

It is Maclean's brother Paul who comes to embody the beautiful. He may be a doomed sinner in the judgment of the world and in the judgment of his father's congregation, but in the eyes of both father and brother he seems redeemed by his beautiful fishing. Early on Paul decided that "he had two major purposes in life: to fish and not to work, or at least not allow work to interfere with fishing" (6). When he became a reporter, writes his brother, "he had come close to realizing life's purposes, which did not conflict in his mind from those given in answer to the first question in *The Westminster Catechism*" (7). Paul could enjoy God by perfecting his chosen art, even while, as a natural man, he entangled himself in affairs and in gambling debts. Within his art, he disciplines himself, lives by the rhythm preached by his father, makes himself worthy of grace.

After he is brutally beaten to death because, it appears, he failed to pay his debts, Paul's father and brother derive some ultimate solace from remembering him as a fisherman. When the father pushes Maclean for more information about Paul's death, the author replies,

> "I've said I've told you all I know. If you push me far enough, all I really know is that he was a fine fisherman."
>
> "You know more than that," my father said. "He was beautiful."
>
> "Yes," I said, "he was beautiful. He should have been— you taught him."
>
> My father looked at me for a long time—he just looked at me. So this was the last he and I ever said to each other about Paul's death. (103)

Paul's beauty may not count much toward heaven in orthodox circles, but if it is informed with God's rhythm, if he has been pious in his art, he may be said to enjoy God forever. It seems the intention of his brother so to say.

A second strain common to the piscatory prose of Thoreau and Maclean reflects an involvement with the natural world befitting anglers. Both men try to synthesize the natural and the supernatural; both consider the possibilities of a natural religion. Walton in his quiet way also celebrates the natural kingdom, wherein "the goodness of the God of *Nature* is manifest" (185—emphasis Walton).

He would not, of course, take nature for God, nor therein ground his faith. His complete angler would be apt to carry his Bible with him to read in solitude by a stream whereas Thoreau's would be more likely to *substitute* his natural activity for Bible study. The Walton of the Concord River fishes as "a sort of solemn sacrament," without biblical sanction or benefit of clergy (*A Week*, 22–23).

Fishing has a part in Thoreau's own sustained sacrament at Walden, in his incorporation of the natural and the supernatural. He tells of dark nights in which his "thoughts wandered to vast and cosmogonal themes in other spheres" until a "faint jerk" on his line in the water linked him once more to the natural sphere. "It seemed," he concludes, "as if I might cast my line upward into the air, as well as downward into this element which was scarcely more dense. Thus I caught two fishes as it were with one hook" (175). His whole life at Walden became one artful hook with which to catch experience, body and soul, to enjoy God forever right now, to attain a perfection in space and time that breaks the boundaries of space and time.

Maclean as well as Thoreau takes seriously Christ's command, "Be ye therefore perfect, even as your father which is in heaven is perfect" (Matt. 5:48). Like Thoreau, he looks to nature for perfection, seeks high moments of integration with a world "perfect and apart" from the messy affairs of men (37). He achieves identity with the river, feels, incorporates its past, future, and present (61–63). He experiences romantic "spots of time" in which "eternity is compressed into a moment," in which all time and space are now and here. One such spot concludes when a big fish he has been trying to land disappears or is transfigured into a bush. "Even Moses," asserts Maclean, "could not have trembled more when his bush blew up on him" (44). His tone suggests that he thinks this episode more comic than romantic or sacramental, but by casting himself as a Montana Moses standing before the natural turned supernatural, Maclean wittily testifies to the religious dimensions of his life and art.

Maclean's aesthetic quest for perfection in nature, for a purely natural religion such as Thoreau sustained himself with, is tempered and qualified by two sets of circumstances, of realities. The realities of fishing often leave him with a tangled line and an empty hook, cutting short those spots of time that should have culminated in a big catch, and confirming the Presbyterian notion of the world of men as a mess. More importantly, the circumstances of human life, the realities, especially, of his brother's story, compel Maclean to look at perfection—and nature—more humanistically. In doing so, he explores the ultimate religious significance of his subject, a significance to be considered in the conclusion of this paper.

The third strain present in Thoreau's writing and "A River Runs Through It" is elegiac. The authors pay tribute to past or passing cultures and to loved ones they have lost. Walton also memorializes old friends, old habits, and an old faith. (Some of the "how to" content common to piscatory prose reflects, I think, the desire to honor and keep alive dying skills.) Thoreau's wild fishermen are a dying breed, remnants of less civilized, populated, and propertied times. Moreover, they remind him of his freer, more natural youth (*A Week*, 21, 33–34; *Walden*, 210–213). In elegizing them, he, in a sense, elegizes himself. Maclean too honors scenes and skills dear to him as a young man. With rough tenderness, he describes a time when one could leave some locally brewed beer in the Blackfoot and some clothes on its shore without worrying about marauding hordes (of, needless to say, bait fishermen) from Great Falls, not to mention the West Coast (57–58, 67). Montana is presented in this story as, paradoxically, violent and pastoral, rugged and innocent—all in all, a "beautiful world" if one could survive (56).

There is not much religious significance to this aspect of the elegiac strain, except in that it seeks to keep old ways and values vital, to keep the faith. The strain runs deeper, however. Thoreau's *A Week* is his elegy for his brother John, with whom he took his river journey, and who now, Thoreau assures himself, ascends "fairer rivers" (2). The death of his brother was a shattering experience for Thoreau, complicated by guilt over not being open enough in his love for him in life, and not being able to rescue him from the grip of lockjaw. Thoreau works out his guilt in his writing, overcomes his doubts about the efficacy of love, and sustains through art his brother's life.

"A River Runs Through It" is an elegy for brother Paul. It tests the efficacy of brotherly love. Brotherly love is a tradition among anglers; Walton traces it back to the brotherhood of fishing disciples surrounding Jesus (28, 46). Maclean centers his concern on a belief or instinct that preceeds the gospel, one which reflects a common situation: "I knew there were others like me who had brothers they did not understand but wanted to help. We are probably those referred to as 'our brothers' keepers,' possessed of one of the oldest and possibly one of the most futile and certainly one of the most haunting of instincts. It will not let us go" (28–29). His concern as his brother's keeper will not let him go as he tries to enter the perfect world fishermen and other artists like to immerse themselves in (37). It eventually fosters a richer understanding of perfection and love, but it fails to keep his brother alive. It appears, indeed, to be one of the most futile of instincts.

Much of Maclean's story deals with his failure to help his brother, who drinks and gambles too much, always desperate, it seems, to prove himself, to stake himself. He won't accept money or advice; the best Maclean can do is go fishing with him, share in an art which Paul has perfected, in which his essential beauty is manifest. A fishing trip provides a "momentary stay against confusion," but it does not settle his gambling debts or bring order out of the confusion of the world beyond the river. A subplot of the story, which has Maclean trying to help a brother-in-law, a prodigal son of Montana turned West Coast debauchee and bait fisherman, appears to reconfirm the failure of brotherly concern: all the brother-in-law gets out of the fishing expedition his sister (Maclean's wife) and mother hope will help him is a lot of whiskey and beer, a bad sunburn, and a whore. Believing Maclean to be in trouble with his wife and mother-in-law over the condition of their burnt-up and burnt-out baby, Paul becomes, in a change of roles, *his* brother's keeper. He organizes a family fishing trip. It is this trip, the last the brothers and their father take together, that, as recollected by Maclean, provides him and the reader with the assurance that brotherly love does have its efficacy, that neither this nor any love is in the long run futile. This trip, furthermore, completes his and our religious education.

*   *   *

It would be helpful, I think, to set the lessons of this, the climactic scene of the story, in the context of the story's genesis. Maclean traces its beginnings to a hot afternoon on the river:

> As the heat mirages on the river in front of me danced with and through each other, I could feel patterns from my own life joining with them. It was here, while waiting for my brother, that I started this story, although, of course, at the time I did not know that stories of life are often more like rivers than books. But I knew a story had begun, perhaps long ago near the sound of water. And I sensed that ahead I would meet something that would never erode so there would be a sharp turn, deep circles, a deposit, and quietness. (63)

Waiting for his brother, he senses the patterns and sounds of the river stimulating and shaping his responses and making available a model for his art. He might have found in Thoreau or elsewhere the conventional analogy between the course of a river and the course of a life, but he could not find in any book, nor did he yet know, the realities of life that do not lend themselves, any more than rivers do, to neat and happy aesthetic or philosophic formulations. Waiting for his brother, he does not have the human realities to work with. When his brother arrives, in love and in death, he does. In one sense, Paul's death is that "something that would never erode," thereby determining the shape of his life and the shape of his brother's story. In another sense, it is love that never erodes, that informs life with significance, that fosters any story worth telling.

Love does not depend on understanding. Father and son agree

on this when, after Paul's death, they struggle to explain what happened: " 'Are you sure you have told me everything you know about his death?' he asked. I said, 'Everything.' 'It's not much, is it?' 'No,' I replied, 'but you can love completely without completely understanding.' 'That I have known and preached,' my father said'' (103). The father does not need to be educated in the gospel—that is his profession. In a later conversation which still reflects the presence of Paul, the father, however, prods his story-telling son toward an easier profession:

"You like to tell true stories, don't you?" he asked, and I answered, "Yes, I like to tell stories that are true."

Then he asked, "After you have finished your true stories sometime, why don't you make up a story and the people to go with it?

"Only then will you understand what happened and why.

"It is those we live with and love and should know who elude us." (104)

Maclean, however, follows his father's practice rather than his advice. He fishes with words for those real and elusive people he has lived with and loved. The result is "A River Runs Through It."

The last family fishing trip is filled with complete acts of love: Paul bringing the family together; Paul hugging his mother, who loves best the son she understands least; Paul rising early to make breakfast after a night on the town; Paul suggesting that he and Maclean fish close together; and Paul wading across the river to give his brother the fly to catch the last fish his brother ever caught in his company. Maclean thinks of these as his finest fish, the fruit of brotherly love (94). Through Paul, Maclean achieves a new definition of "finest," a more humanistic understanding of perfection which humanizes his art.

The author is satisfied with his day's catch. While waiting for Paul to fish his limit, which he always does as if to fulfill the law,

Maclean searches out his father, whom he rightly suspects is finished fishing and reading the gospel. When the preacher comments on the biblical passage he has been pondering, a dispute ensues:

> "In the part I was reading, it says the Word was in the beginning, and that's right. I used to think water was first, but if you listen carefully you will hear that the words are underneath the water."
>
> "That's because you are a preacher first and then a fisherman," I told him. "If you ask Paul, he will tell you that the words are formed out of water."
>
> "No," my father said, "you are not listening carefully. The water runs over the words. Paul will tell you the same thing." (95–96)

The father affirms the assertion of the first verse of John: Logos, the Word—Reason, Spirit—precedes and informs the material world, is its life, its rhythm, its significance. He has come to believe in the primacy of meaning. We are not told what meaning he discerns in the words underneath the water. That is left to our imagination and religion.

The young Maclean feels his father is biased because he lives by words, and thinks Paul, a man of action, who lives most fully when fishing the water, will support the liberal, empiricist, naturalistic position he himself apparently holds. The father thinks not. We never hear from Paul on the subject; his last words in the story announce his not-to-be-honored wish for three more years to perfect his ability to think like a fish, to perfect an art which his father and brother already see as perfectly beautiful. Why is the father sure that his younger, somewhat prodigal son shares his faith? Perhaps the key is "carefully," a word the father emphasizes through repetition. A man who carefully, religiously devotes himself to his natural sphere of action, as Paul does when fishing, concludes, or knows without concluding, that within this sphere there is a rhythm, a rightness, a Word which comes to inform his art.

The conclusion of "A River Runs Through It" suggests this, and suggests that Maclean has listened carefully for a long time, heard the words, and been converted to the faith of his father and brother:

> Now nearly all those I loved and did not understand when I was young are dead, but I still reach out to them.
>
> Of course, now I am too old to be much of a fisherman, and now of course I usually fish the big waters alone, although some friends think I shouldn't. Like many fly fishermen in western Montana where the summer days are almost Arctic in length, I often do not start fishing until the cool of the evening. Then in the Arctic half-light of the canyon, all existence fades to a being with my soul and memories and the sounds of the Big Blackfoot River and a four-count rhythm and the hope that a fish will rise.
>
> Eventually, all things merge into one, and a river runs through it. The river was cut by the world's great flood and runs over rocks from the basement of time. On some of the rocks are timeless raindrops. Under the rocks are the words and some of the words are theirs.
>
> I am haunted by waters. (104)

Maclean leaves us reaching and fishing, fishing and writing. He leaves us in hope and he leaves us haunted. He has explored the basement of time and found timeless raindrops. As timeless as the raindrops are the words under the rocks.

Whose words? There is some difficulty in catching the antecedent of "theirs." Logical antecedents are "rocks" and "raindrops"; they make natural sense. It is, however, human sense that Maclean has been making. I propose leaping up two paragraphs to those he loves, to those he has been trying to reach. Some of the words, I think, are theirs. More especially, it is his father and brother to whom he has been listening carefully. They offer him the words of life. Not the Word, but the words. Like the waters that haunt Maclean, the Word assumes a multitude of forms, including human. Men and women contribute their own words, help bring the world into significance. The author, a sign broker by profession, is fundamentally humanistic, as is his art. Nevertheless, reaching out to loved ones and reaching out to readers, he follows a high religious calling: Maclean is a fisher of men.

WORKS CITED

Maclean, Norman. *A River Runs Through It and Other Stories*. Chicago, University of Chicago Press, 1976.
Thoreau, Henry David. *Walden*. Princeton: Princeton University Press, 1971.
Thoreau, Henry David. *A Week on the Concord and Merrimack Rivers*. Boston: Houghton Mifflin Co., 1906.
Walton, Isaac. *The Compleat Angler*. New York: Collier Books, 1962.

Common Texts

Gordon G. Brittan, Jr.*

Talk with someone who teaches the Humanities long enough, and eventually he or she will mention a book. Our experience is largely, although of course not entirely, of the book-side of things. We form communities of readers.

People who have read the same books belong to the same communities. They share something in common, a particular experience or idea, made uncommon by some author's having expressed it in a certain way.

It is simply a fact, I think, that to the extent that we have read the same books, and by virtue of this shared experience or idea and its expression, we can communicate more fully with one another, at the very least being able to presuppose common meanings and a wider range of associations.

⁎ ⁎ ⁎

*"Common Texts" by Gordon Brittan, Jr. is reprinted from the text of the Montana State University Honors Lecture he delivered on June 14, 1985. Copyright © 1985 by Gordon Brittan, Jr.

What worries me at the moment is the restricted opportunity for communication across our culture.

Admittedly my perspective is both limited and somewhat biased. After all, I teach reading and writing for a living. And, like other teachers of the Humanities, I have felt increasingly isolated from areas of contemporary concern, not as a citizen but as a teacher.

I think we lose in very important ways as members of a culture who no longer have a common bond of literacy between them, who cannot, for example, any longer summarize a complex of thought and feeling with a single reference to *Hamlet*, of whose mental and imaginative frontiers are restricted to their own experiences.

Well, what are we going to do?

*   *   *

What I suggest is that we make increased use of our regional authors, in our case encouraging the reading of and responding to a very extensive Montana literature. Books by A. B. Guthrie and Dorothy Johnson, of course, but more recently others by Ivan Doig, Spike Van Cleve, and Norman Maclean, to name a few. These authors and their books still matter, still make a difference to people living here and elsewhere. They are accessible insofar as they illuminate in an uncommon way a landscape, events, and styles of life that are common to many of us, indeed some so close at hand that but for this illumination we would have missed their meaning, their humor, their beauty, and their sadness. They go some way toward showing us who and what we are, not surprising since we are as much reflections of the books we read as they are of us and our forefathers. My guess is that all of us in this room are linked by one or more of these books, that I can make real contact with you, at last, by mentioning one of their names, that you remember, as I do, some special insight or emotion you had in reading them. We can take them as our common texts. What's crucial is that the best of them sustain prolonged reflection. They are ''regional'' only in the most accidental sense of the word. Like all good reading, they take us outside ourselves, leaving us at moments drained, dazed, and happy.

Of all the books I might mention, the one that has been most important for me is Norman Maclean's *A River Runs Through It*. By anyone's standards, he is a legend and it is a classic. If by some strange quirk of fate you haven't already done so, I'm now going to persuade you to read it.

A River Runs Through It is Maclean's memoir, unsentimental and moving, of days some 50 years ago or so spent in and around fly-fishing some streams in western Montana with his brother Paul and his father, a Scot and Presbyterian minister in Missoula who drew no clear line between fly-fishing and religion. But it is also a great deal more.

In the attempt to say what more, allow me to look with you at a couple of passages.

The river that runs through it is the Big Blackfoot. In some sense it is both the center and the image of their lives, a symbol of time, of change, but also something permanent. Maclean is sitting on its banks, a young man, finished with his fishing, looking at the river, trying to forget the brother-in-law and his dubious woman friend who have tagged along, drunk the beer, and almost ruined the day.

> I sat there and forgot and forgot, until what remained was the river that went by and I who watched. On the river the heat mirages danced with each other and then they danced through each other and then they joined hands and danced around each other. Eventually the watcher joined the river, and there was only one of us.

To which Maclean adds humorously, "I believe it was the river." At least it was a selfless moment.

With all content removed, he begins to reflect on the river's form.

> Not far downstream was a dry channel where the river had run once, and part of the way to come to know a thing is through its death. But years ago I had known the river

when it flowed through this now dry channel, so I could
enliven its stony remains with the waters of memory.

In death, the form is fixed, whether of a thing or of a person, as it
is of the past, which is also dead and gone. But the past can be
recovered, reconstituted, and brought to life in memory.

> In death it had its pattern, and we can only hope for as
> much. Its overall pattern was the favorite serpentine curve
> of the artist sketched in the valley from my hill to the last
> hill I could see on the other side. But internally it was made
> of sharp angles. It ran seemingly straight for a while,
> turned abruptly, then ran smoothly again, then met an-
> other obstacle, again was turned sharply and again ran
> smoothly. Straight lines that couldn't be exactly straight
> and angles that couldn't have been exactly right angles
> became the artist's most beautiful curve and swept from
> here across the valley to where it could be no longer seen.

We can only hope for pattern or form because nowhere else is there
coherence or significance. But this pattern is not simply found; it is
also imposed. The smooth serpentine curve of the artist is contrasted
with the crooked lines and sharp angles of the river itself. There are
no perfect forms in nature. We derive them only by an effort of
abstraction.

Maclean doesn't so much *tell* us there's a pattern as *show* us the
pattern. The pattern is in his sentences, of course, but more especially in their rhythm and their sound. Notice how the rough rhythm
of ''Straight lines that couldn't be exactly straight and angles that
couldn't have been exactly right angles'' (it's difficult to read these
words without stumbling) gives way, mid-sentence, to the smooth
and flowing ''became the artist's most beautiful curve and swept
from here across the valley. . . .'' To say that Maclean is a great
story-teller is to suggest many things, but it is first to insist that the
stories be read with the ear. At one point, we are told about how
fishermen ''read'' the water. But mainly we are supposed to listen

to the river, to the words, and more especially to the voices and
their cadences.

Story-telling is also teaching, Maclean likes to say, and here as
elsewhere he draws on his knowledge of geology to take us inside
the river and to deepen our understanding and appreciation of its
form. For what is knowledge but knowledge of form?

> The Big Blackfoot is a new glacial river that runs and
> drops fast. The river is a straight rapids until it strikes big
> rocks or big trees with big roots. This is the turn that is
> not exactly at right angles. Then it swirls and deepens
> among big rocks and circles back through them where big
> fish live under the foam. As it slows, the sand and small
> rocks it picked up in the fast rapids above begin to settle
> out and are deposited and the water becomes shallow and
> quiet. After the deposit is completed, it starts running
> again.

Finally, Maclean rejoins the river, generalizing this pattern to include his own:

> As the heat mirages in front of me danced with and
> through each other, I could feel patterns from my own life
> joining with them. It was here, while waiting for my
> brother, that I started this story, although, of course, at
> the time I did not know that stories of life are often more
> like rivers than books. But I knew a story had begun, per-
> haps long ago near the sound of water. And I sensed that
> ahead I would meet something that would never erode so
> that there would be a sharp turn, deep circles, a deposit,
> and quietness.

This is an important moment in the narrative. Life for the first time
within it begins to take on the coherence of literature. For it is, after
all, only in telling a story, about our own lives and those of others,
that form begins to emerge, that events follow one another with a

certain inevitability, that there is a beginning and an end; and that
we start to see significance. Such story-telling is always after the
fact; lived experience is for the most part formless and without
meaning. Only later do we begin to discover patterns, unities, but
only as we begin, in this case as an old man, to recover that experience in memory and order it in words.

I've spent a long time with this passage, quoting much of it. For
it seems to me to be a perfect example of the patterns about which
Maclean is speaking, moving symmetrically from the initial
thoughtless merging of writer and river, observer and observed, to
reflections on ways in which the writer's forms are and correspond
to the river's to a thoughtful re-merging of writer and river through
the discovery of a new pattern, a story, that embraces both of them.
And, of course, I am very much interested, as a philosopher, in
forms, in the shapes of things, and in whether we find or create
them. But I've hardly begun to do it justice, there's so much richness and complexity. The best we teachers of the Humanities can
do, in the final analysis so to speak, is to efface ourselves and direct
attention to the text. And hope that the experience of sitting on a
hot afternoon in the 1930's on the banks of the Big Blackfoot, the
rhythm of the river, the insight into pattern, meaning, and memory,
the feeling of perfect integration, between man and nature, life and
literature, is shared. Brought to see the universal in particular, we
sense a certain possibility for ourselves.

A second passage, toward the end of the story, has more to do
with the Calvinist than the Aristotelian Maclean. I'll be much briefer
this time. Again we're on the banks of the Big Blackfoot. Maclean
and his father are sitting together at the end of another day, watching Paul demonstrate all his power and artistry in the catching of
one last big fish, a copy of the Greek New Testament by their side.
It's too deep for Paul to wade across, so tucking his cigarettes and
matches in his hat, he starts to swim:

> My father and I sat on the bank and laughed at each
> other. It never occurred to either of us to hurry to the shore
> in case he needed help with a rod in his right hand and a

basket loaded with fish on his left shoulder. In our family it was no great thing for a fisherman to swim a river with matches in his hair. We laughed at each other because we knew he was getting damn good and wet, and we lived in him, and were swept over the rocks with him and held his rod high in one of our hands.

We're swept along too. That's the gift of the great story-teller, to bring his listeners into the story, especially when he's trying to teach them something, even something difficult like the 4-beat rhythm of a cast. This is the Paul they understand, in whom they do not merely live but exist. But there is another Paul whom they do not understand, a son and brother who is a creature of passion and can't come to terms with his own violence and is found beaten to death in an alley. Maclean gives us to understand that Paul had somehow fallen from grace and was beyond salvation by anyone, though not beyond their love. At the same time, although grace can never be recovered much less earned, Paul is a figure of grace, at least standing in the Big Blackfoot with a fly rod in his hand. "To him," Maclean says of his father, "all good things—trout as well as eternal salvation—come by grace and grace comes by art and art does not come easy." This, I suppose, was the riddle, some form of the problem of evil: Paul was graceful and could be understood and Paul was damned and beyond all human comprehension. The most that could be made of his life was to find or create a pattern that, even if it left some things, as it must, incomprehensible, restored Paul's grace by an art that is effortless and did not come easy.

For a very long time, I worried about the social significance of my teaching. Reading the philosophy texts which are my specialty, mainly from the 17th and 18th centuries, day after day, year after year—what did they have to do with eliminating the threat of nuclear war, or ending the African famine, or aiding the fight for social justice? Nothing, apparently.

But reflecting on the concrete reality of my reading, I have slowly come to see that there is something to it after all. Two things, in fact.

One of them has to do with community. I try to help form communities of readers around particular common texts, and beyond that around the long tradition that constitutes western civilization. These are living communities, felt as much as thought, resting on shared experiences and shared expressions and rooted in a common language. In a way, they are ideal communities, involving a communion between writers and readers stretching over time which transcends any sort of social relations, and invoking mutual trust. These communities are, I think, basic, presupposed by the political and economic communities to which we otherwise belong. It was for this reason that Jefferson put such stress on the creation of a ''common reader'' within our culture.

Communities of the book, communities within the book. Norman, Paul, their father, their wives, mothers, and girl-friends form a community, individuals like ourselves reaching out to one another, intermittently making contact, bound by common interests, psychological conflicts and love.

The other thing has to do with possibility. In reading texts together we not only share experiences, but become self-conscious about the ways in which they are expressed. There is nothing inevitable about forms. Here are some, there are others. But realizing the diversity of forms into which our experience has been cast traditionally, we are free to experiment with others, to create new forms. We have to know where the limits of our language lie if we are to go beyond them.

There is also more immediately and directly human possibility. In reading we go well beyond the range of ordinary experience, to possibilities only imagined. We see the dark side of human nature, Paul's self-destructive tendencies, but we are also exposed to the possibilities of grace.

Possibility and community, these are the watchwords. My hope is that my students will realize the deep sources of their communities and the vast extent of their possibilities and in the process discover not only why but how our world should be redeemed.

Mo-nah-se-tah, the Whore, and the Three Scottish Women

Mary Clearman Blew*

Very early in the title novella of *A River Runs Through It*, Norman Maclean reveals, in a single scene, a glimpse of a woman so compelling that her image refuses to fade even though she hardly is mentioned again:

> His girl was sitting on the floor at his feet. . . . Looking down on her now I could see only the spread of her hair on her shoulders and the spread of her legs on the floor. Her hair did not glisten and I had never seen her legs when they were just things lying on a floor. Knowing that I was looking down on her, she struggled to get to her feet, but her long legs buckled and her stockings slipped down on her legs and she spread out on the floor again until the tops of her stockings and her garters showed. (25–26)

So carefully does Maclean arrange this scene, indeed so carefully does he present *A River Runs Through It* as heightened memory, as

*This essay was written especially for this volume and appears here for the first time with the permission of the author.

true, that it is at once familiar and disturbing to recognize in his snapshot of the Northern Cheyenne girl drunk and degraded on the floor of the jail at the feet of Maclean's brother, Paul, not only a real girl as, apparently, recalled exactly by Maclean, but also one of the sensual and destructive Dark Women out of the mainstream of American fiction: Cooper's Cora or Judith; Hawthorne's Hester, Miriam, or Zenobia; Poe's Ligeia and Twain's Roxana. Indeed, Maclean's Northern Cheyenne girl shares so many of the characteristics of these fictional antecedents that the crucial ways in which she differs from them seem at first obscure.

To begin, she is endowed with a beauty like theirs, and particularly the beauty of her hair, which Maclean lingers over in language reminiscent of Hawthorne: "When her black hair glistened, she was one of my favorite women . . . . when her hair glistened . . . she was worth it" (25–26). And she is dark in coloring, a trait which the earlier writers used as an emblem not only of a terrifying capacity for passion but also of a dark heritage which carries with it the threat, or "taint," as Cooper would have called it, of miscegenation. "Mo-nah-se-tah," Maclean nicknames her, a nickname he says she "took to" only after she learned its true significance as the name of the Cheyenne girl who was Custer's mistress and who was said to have borne his son.

Like other Dark Women, the Northern Cheyenne girl has a claim of her own to artistry: "She was one of the most beautiful dancers I have ever seen. She made her partner feel as if he were about to be left behind, or already had been. . . . She was as beautiful a dancer as (Paul) was a fly caster" (26). Her claim to artistry is, in other words, as great as Paul's; she is, in this respect at least, an equal and fitting mate for Maclean's flawed brother whose genius haunts the novella.

Finally and pointedly, like the earlier Dark Women, she is dangerous. She is dangerous not only because she can stir passion and respond to it, or because she carries within her the old threat of the woman of a primitive race luring the white-skinned man away from civilization and its moral restraints, or even, on the most basic level, because of her relish for starting street fights or for drinking. Rather,

she is a threat in a way Maclean establishes explicitly in the story
of her Cheyenne great-grandmother, who helped cut the testicles off
Custer's still living troopers, and implicitly in the one direct glimpse
he allows of her, drunken and stinking in jail, her wonderful long
legs reduced to "just things lying on a floor." The legs themselves
are a further clue, as Leslie Fiedler has remarked of another degraded *anima*, "those improbable legs which America has bred onto
the naturally short-legged female form to symbolize castrating
power" (317). By now it should be clear that the Northern Cheyenne girl's portrait is drawn from more than heightened memory.
Indeed, after such a powerful evocation of the Dark Woman of
American fiction, any reader might be excused for expecting to have
found, here in the early pages of the novella, a potential solution to
the disturbing question at its core; the question, that is, of Mac-
clean's brother Paul. The Northern Cheyenne girl is, surely, Paul's
Bad Angel. (Maclean himself has been saved from committing the
worst of Paul's sins, from this point of view, by marrying a good
Scotch-Irish girl.) On one level, the Northern Cheyenne girl is the
bad girl, the bad influence, any son's mother's nightmare, who
leads Paul on drinking bouts and gets him into fights. On another
level, from this same point of view, she is a projection of Paul's
worst impulses, his *anima*, the dark side of his heart in contrast to
the side of him reflected in the sparkling waters of the trout rivers.
Lending credence to this reading is the shame Paul shows when
Maclean comes to get him and his girl out of jail: "his enlarged
casting hand was over his face. . . . His overdeveloped right wrist
held his right hand over his eyes so that in some drunken way he
thought I could not see him" (25–27).

One indication, however, that such a reading ultimately is unsatisfactory is the Northern Cheyenne girl's subsequent disappearance
from the novella. She is allowed no space to develop either into
temptress or projection of dark impulses, but rather is left as a kind
of accoutrement of Paul's, taken up briefly and dropped. She is the
kind of dangerous woman a man like Paul might squire around
town as a token of his own toughness. Going out with an Indian in
Montana of the nineteen-thirties, where Indians could not at that

time legally live within the city limits of the state capitol, and where anti-miscegenation laws lingered into the nineteen-fifties, is a gesture as provocative as getting in the first punch in a street fight.

Another indication that the Northern Cheyenne girl is at the same time both more or less than the Dark Woman of American fiction lies in the fact of Paul's shame itself. What, one finally has to ask, is he ashamed of? Certainly not of his girl. Certainly not of punching the man who leaned out of a restaurant booth and yelled "Wahoo!" as they walked by. Certainly not of going out with an Indian even in, especially in, Montana in 1937. Maclean himself supports all these actions up to a point.

> The sergeant said, "The guy said to me, 'Jesus, all I meant is that it's funny to go out with an Indian. It was just a joke.'"

> I said to the sergeant, "it's not very funny," and the sergeant said, "No, not very funny, but it's going to cost your brother a lot of money and time to get out of it. What really isn't funny is that he's behind in the game at Hot Springs. Can't you help him straighten out?" (24)

Paul, one concludes, is ashamed of himself in defeat. The tough Montana boy has bet on himself and lost; true, against impossibly high odds, but defeated all the same in the big stud poker game, in the restaurant fight, in the streets. Most humiliating of all, he has been exposed in defeat before the brother whose life is diverging so far from his.

The Northern Cheyenne girl, meanwhile, has followed a course curiously parallel to Paul's. The descendent of women who castrated Custer's troopers has been reduced to life in a camp next to a slaughterhouse and to the ultimate sordidness, described in sexually charged language like "the spread of her legs," of the jail floor. As tough a woman as Paul is a man, she has been pitted against the inexorable forces of a civilization that avenged Custer, wiped out the culture of the Northern Cheyennes along with the rest of the Indians in Montana, and eventually will pollute the beauty of the Big Blackfoot River. The odds against her as well as Paul have been impossibly high; the dancer has been overcome by the dance.

As for Maclean, he is ashamed of them both: "They smelled just like what they were," he says, "a couple of drunks whose stomachs had been injected with whatever it is the body makes when it feels cold and full of booze and knows something bad has happened and doesn't want tomorrow to come" (26). He does not, however, assign extra blame to the Northern Cheyenne girl for leading the dance to the gutter; she and Paul may have reached the brink together, but they have each fallen on their own, and in fact Maclean gives the girl the final judgment of the episode (and her last words in the novella): "He should have killed the bastard," she says just before she passes out (27).

After her disappearance from the novella, the Northern Cheyenne girl is replaced in several respects by a character who corresponds more nearly than she to an American fictional type. A sizable portion of narrative and dramatic interest, along with the role of Bad Angel to a mother's son, is taken over by the whore of Wolf Creek, Old Rawhide.

Like the Northern Cheyenne girl, Old Rawhide is described as strong, aggressive, and attractive. Unlike her, she is white (an early indication that she is much more closely related to the blonde American bitches of Fitzgerald and Hemingway than to the Dark Woman of the older fictional tradition); and unlike her, she invades the exclusively male and sacred preserve of the trout rivers in a particularly blasphemous way. Perhaps because of the latter incursion, during which she violates the sacrament of fly fishing by bringing along a bait can, drinking all the beer, and seducing his brother-in-law on a sandbar in the middle of the Big Blackfoot River, Maclean denies her even the qualified respect he showed the Northern Cheyenne girl. His contempt for her is barely relieved by humor:

> About ten years before, at a Fourth of July celebration, she had been elected beauty queen of Wolf Creek. She had

ridden bareback standing up through the 111 inhabitants, mostly male, who had lined one of Wolf Creek's two streets. Her skirts flew high, and she won the contest. But, since she didn't have what it takes to become a professional rider, she did the next best thing. However, she still wore the divided skirts of a western horsewoman of the day, although they must have been a handicap in her new profession. (31)

Where Maclean gave his Dark Woman a certain integrity of her own and linked her, through her defeat, to the spiritual values associated with the trout rivers, he explicitly depicts Old Rawhide as corrupt. As anti-virgin, she has aligned herself with the social forces that have turned over the Big Blackfoot River from a private paradise to "dude ranches, the unselected inhabitants of Great Falls, and the Moorish invaders from California" (13). If the Northern Cheyenne girl looks back to a violent but essentially innocent past, Old Rawhide looks ahead to a violent and banal future.

The image of woman as anti-virgin recurs in Maclean's fiction, always in association with male weakness. She is present in the whores of Hamilton in "USFS 1919: The Ranger, the Cook, and a Hole in the Sky," against whose malignancy the young Norman invokes the protection of iambs, like a Celtic satirist's charms, and whose rapacity ultimately exposes the fraudulence of the card-shark cook. In "Logging and Pimping, and 'Your Pal, Jim,' " she appears as the "Southern" whores who personify the antagonist's limitations and with him create "a warm family circle of lies" (122).

So it also is that, by aligning herself with Maclean's passive brother-in-law, who fishes with bait, that Old Rawhide is revealed as Bad Angel. Clearly the aggressor in the relationship with Neal, who early has learned the power of passivity in manipulating his mother and sister, Old Rawhide further unmans him with her strength. Although Neal already has been revealed as a poseur and a bad liar who tries to claim the wilderness values he cannot begin to comprehend or live up to, Old Rawhide humiliates him during the sandbar episode to the point that he virtually becomes catatonic.

First, by seducing Neal under the full glare of the sun on the river, Old Rawhide not only parodies the theme of love which dominates the novella, but also exposes Neal: literally, he is exposed to sunburn, and metaphorically, to the stripping away of his last claims to dignity. She degrades him with her promiscuity, propositioning Maclean and Paul over his limp body. She shames him with her strength, helping him to wade through the swift current from sandbar to shore—"The man couldn't have made it without the strength in her legs," Maclean acknowledges (70). Finally, and without an inkling of its significance, she retrieves for him the red Hills Bros. coffee can that has become a kind of scarlet letter for bait fishermen and Neal's special badge of inadequacy. At the conclusion of the episode, Neal, lacking even the strength to pull up his pants by himself, is delivered over to his mother and sister in a state approaching the infantile.

It is Paul, however, and not Neal that Old Rawhide recognizes as her true adversary. In this respect she differs dramatically from Bad Angels in Maclean's other fiction. Unlike the whores of Hamilton, Old Rawhide refuses to snarl from the confines of the crib or to content herself with robbing a man already exposed as counterfeit. Nor, like the "Southern" whores, is she a faceless extension of a pimp. Old Rawhide, aggressive in her own context, pits her toughness against Paul's toughness, her banality against his artistry, the perversion she represents against his special ability to worship at the inmost shrine of the trout rivers. But it really is no contest; here, at least, the victory is Paul's. When he kicks her squarely in the source of her perversion, right between the LO and the VE tattooed on her buttocks, Maclean leaves no doubt about his own stance:

> Suddenly, I developed a passion to kick a woman in the ass. I was never aware of such a passion before, but now it overcame me. I jumped out of the car, and caught up to her, but she had been kicked in the ass before and by experts, so I missed her completely. Still, I felt better for the effort. (73)

That Paul's triumph will be brief already has been foreshadowed. Neither does his rout of Old Rawhide answer the unresolved questions about Paul. Maclean's gloss suggests that, to Paul, defeating Old Rawhide is meaningless. "Much as he hated her, he really had no strong feeling about her. It was the bastard in the back seat without any underwear that he hated . . . (Neal) who was untouchable because of three Scotch women" (72).

The three Scottish women are more formidable by far than either the Northern Cheyenne girl or Old Rawhide. Mother, sister, and sister-in-law to Neal; wife, mother-in-law, and sister-in-law to Maclean, they are presented consistently as a unified force, as a trinity. Neal, although under their protection, is terrified of them. "I don't want to see three women" (71), he keeps whimpering during the drive home from the ill-fated fishing trip, and Maclean silently adds, "I didn't want to see three women either" (71).

The Scottish women's strength is drawn from familiar sources. Never intruding upon the exclusively male territory of the trout rivers, they hold absolute sway over their traditional domestic and social preserves. They practice the healing arts—"the three of them were thought of as the medical center of Wolf Creek" (35)—and preside over the complexities of familial ties and their Scottish and Presbyterian heritage. Theirs is the combined authority of blood, custom, and church.

These are not their only sources of strength. Elsewhere Maclean has painted the fate of a Presbyterian woman, "a big woman on a big horse" (115), who becomes the object of the ferocious lumberjack of "Logging and Pimping and 'Your Pal, Jim.' " He seduces her to a chorus of ribaldry from the entire logging camp, humiliates her—"By late afternoon she rode back into camp. She never stopped. She was hurried and at a distance looked white and didn't have any huckleberries. She didn't even have her empty pail" (116). Indeed, humiliation alone is not punishment enough; for her fall, Maclean disallows all sympathy:

> At first I felt kind of sorry for her because she was so well known in camp and was so much talked about, but

she was riding "High, Wide, and Handsome." She was
back in camp every Sunday. She always came with a gallon
pail and she always left without it. (116)

"Logging and Pimping and 'Your Pal, Jim,' " however, is a
story of inadequacies masked by humor. The distance between it
and the novella, like the difference between the Presbyterian woman's abandoned pail and the red coffee can Old Rawhide wades the
Blackfoot River to retrieve, is the distance between weakness and
strength. The three Scottish women of the novella draw strength
from sources far beyond the conventional ones of the Presbyterian
woman on the big horse.

One of these sources is their solidarity. Typifying regional western painting and narrative, where white women often are depicted
as members of a group, where what they represent is emphasized
over their individuality, the three Scottish women emerge separately
only once, at a point crucial for Maclean, to speak in individual
voices. Nor does Maclean render them separately visually, as he
does Old Rawhide or the Northern Cheyenne girl, in one of his
vivid snapshots of frozen action. As a trinity, however, the three
Scottish women loom up from the depths of nightmare with a force
worthy of the Northern Cheyenne girl's great-grandmother:

> The truck emerged out of the storm as if out of the pi-
> oneer past, looking like a covered wagon besieged by cir-
> cling rain. . . .

> First it was the women who appeared and then the mat-
> tress, the women appearing first because two of them held
> carving knives and the other, my wife, held a long fork,
> all of which glittered in the semidarkness under the tarps.
> The women squatted on the floor of the box, and had been
> making sandwiches until they saw my head appear like a
> target on canvas. Then they pointed their cutlery at me.
> (48)

It is a male glimpse into the female mysteries—one might almost say, into the coven. To understand its significance for Maclean and the answer it provides to the mystery of Paul, it is helpful to note how the three Scottish women have sapped Neal's strength, but also how they lend their own strength to Maclean.

Maclean points on several occasions to Neal's mother as the source of his inadequacy. The straw suitcase which belonged to his mother and which held all Neal took out of Montana and all he brought back, is one example; his mother cries at the sight of it. Another example is Neal's habit of manipulating women. Certainly in the coven scene in the back of the truck, Maclean is explicit:

> . . . it took some time for my eyes to get adjusted to my
> brother-in-law lying on the mattress. The light first picked
> up his brow, which was serene but pale, as mine would
> have been if my mother had spent her life in making me
> sandwiches and protecting me from reality. (49)

The unmanning of Neal clearly began long before he met Old Rawhide. However, Maclean just as clearly regards the three Scottish women and the established culture they represent, not necessarily as foes of male freedom and potency, but rather as a rare source of love and courage for the man who is strong enough to receive it. Neal, weak in himself, is undone by their implacable love; but Maclean, face to face with each of them consecutively in the one scene where they emerge as individual women, is rewarded by their love. It is a scene unparalleled in the American fiction tradition from which "A River Runs Through It" springs. One could not imagine a Hemingway protagonist accepting these declarations of love, any more than one could discover a Nick Adams, say, walking out of the wilderness as the adolescent Maclean does in "USFS 1919: The Ranger, the Cook, and a Hole in the Sky," and carrying with him like talismen the values of his father the Presbyterian minister and his mother the poet.

"I love you," says each of the three Scottish women to Maclean in turn, and "never lose touch with me," says his wife. "And we never have," Maclean notes, "although her death has come between us" (77). Buoyed by these avowals of love, Maclean returns to his parents, his brother, and the Big Blackfoot River where, "on this wonderful afternoon when all things came together, it took me one cast, one fish, and some reluctantly accepted advice to attain perfection" (88).

It is a perfection denied his brother, Paul, however unparalleled the artistry of his fly casting. "Just give me three more years" (102), Paul asks, but he will not be given them. Early the following spring, Maclean must tell his parents that Paul has been beaten to death, all the bones in his casting hand broken, and his body dumped in an alley.

To the tragedy of Paul, Maclean offers no easy answers, although he and his parents search for understanding, and at one point his father even ventures, like an echo of Neal's family, "Do you think your mother helps him by buttering his rolls?" (87). But if Neal's spineless acquiescence is not Paul's, neither is his the capacity of Maclean's to receive love. In a world split between male and female, Paul seems curiously unable to achieve wholeness. Whether his is original sin or flawed pride, he is unable to accept succor from any source outside himself.

For Maclean, on the other hand, drawing as he does from the powers of the trout rivers as well as those of blood and custom, the story is a fiction—that is, a story that is true, a way of understanding the truth. And it is a comedy—a healing, a reconciliation, a wholeness achieved through the love of trout rivers and the love of family, an integration completed by the Northern Cheyenne girl, Old Rawhide, and the three Scottish women.

WORKS CITED

Maclean, Norman. *A River Runs Through It and Other Stories*. Chicago: University of Chicago Press, 1976.

On the Sublime
and the Beautiful:
Montana, Longinus, and
Professor Norman Maclean

Glen A. Love*

At some point during my first reading of *A River Runs Through It and Other Stories*—perhaps in the tale of Jim Grierson, the tough logger whose summer and winter lives seemed so incongruous—I can remember wondering how the two halves of the author's life cohered. A professor of English holding an endowed chair at a distinguished metropolitan university who wrote wonderful autobiographical stories in his retirement years, and a boy and young man formed in the Montana mountains and woods, logging and working for the U. S. Forest Service and fly-fishing on the Big Blackfoot River with his brother and their Scottish Presbyterian minister father. I have read Norman Maclean's book with increasing pleasure several times since that first reading, and have introduced it to many of my students in American literature, and I have not lost my curiosity about this figure who so ably spans two different worlds.

At least two sets of literary contrasts are at work in what I have been describing: the contrasts between West and East, country and city, nature and civilization on the one hand, and those between

*This essay was written especially for this volume and appears here for the first time with the permission of the author.

youth and age, heart and head, energy and wisdom, naivete and tragic awareness on the other. These patterns of opposition are, of course, not unfamiliar to readers. The *Bildungsroman* has characteristically depicted the shock of experience upon impressionable and searching innocence; and the pastoral has for centuries recorded the progress of the youth from the provinces who comes to the metropolis but continues to measure his life by the standards derived from the green world of his past. American readers may recognize a more indigenous figure in Maclean's work. That is the peculiarly American type—born out of Melville, Whitman, Twain, Crane, London, Hemingway, Mailer, and countless others—of what has been called the sensitive roughneck, the young man who has been around, but whose perceptive and reflective qualities open his world to the interests of a larger audience. Still, even within these recognizable traditions, Maclean's achievement seems compelling to me, partly because of the extent to which it stretches these patterns of contrast to their extremes. Here was a life a good deal more dramatically divided than could be described by the characteristic American stance of the tender tough guy, or by the comfortable oppositions of the English country gentleman, whose "All winter in the study, all summer in the field" balanced neatly as a golden mean. It is a unique and startling distance, among the lives of our writers, between gyppo logging and a University of Chicago chair in literature.

Maclean's work gathers interest and complexity from another set of opposites, that is from the extremes of time which it encompasses. Not having begun to write stories until he was the age of seventy— surely another American literary record—and looking back to his early years, Maclean invests his fiction with a distinctive quality of wonder and sagacity, a memorable blend of youthful dreams, Montana horse-sense, and the varied reflections of his long life. Writing of this aspect of *A River Runs Through It*, John Cawelti thoughtfully notes that the stories

> . . . are like memories which have been revolved in the mind throughout a lifetime until their hidden truths have been brought to the surface and revealed. Thus there is a

wonderful interplay between the consciousness of the old man telling us the stories and the perspective of the boy of over half a century ago. We see not only what the boy thought or failed to think, but how he began to understand his life and something of what that boy, as a man in his 70's, has made of it since. (25)

As in Cooper's Leatherstocking series, Maclean's character grows ever younger as the stories progress, but his youth at the end of the last story reflects not so much the sloughing off of age which D. H. Lawrence found in Natty Bumppo's youthful emergence, but rather a kind of distillation of the experience of both youth and age, and of the mutually enriching perspectives of each.

Faced with these kinds of contrasts, then, one may be tempted, as I have been, to find connections between the sage and the stripling, between the rapt stories of a western youth and the teller's life as a scholar and intellectual. I hope that Norman Maclean will not find this sort of inquiry impertinent. As he cites one purpose of his book in his introduction, that of letting his "children know what kind of people their parents are or think they are or hope they are," so it is inevitable that his appreciative readers will seek to extend that sort of awareness, thus enhancing the pleasure of what are now their stories as well (ix). Then, too, as the author has included scholars among those for whom these stories are intended, he knows what to expect from these most burrowing of readers (xiv). Eventually, as he says, all things merge into one. And the river which runs through it may have its ideational as well as its physical and spiritual existence. How do the words and ideas of the author's intellectual life flow into his haunting waters?

In approaching some of the scholarly undercurrents of these stories one might begin by citing smaller and more discrete features of the prose, such as literary allusions. There seem to be relatively few of these, for a professor's book, but they're carefully patterned, moving, for example, in the first, title story, from the comic to the serious and philosophical. Early in the story we learn that Isaac Walton " 'is not a respectable writer. He was an Episcopalian and a bait fisherman.' '' Thus cautions Maclean's father to his sons, while brother Paul privately confides to the narrator, after locating a copy of *The Compleat Angler*, that '' 'the bastard doesn't even know how to spell "complete." ' '' The narrator finds some of Walton's songs to dairymaids appealing, but cannot shake realist Paul's scornful opinion, '' 'Whoever saw a dairymaid on the Big Blackfoot River?' ''(5). But this first story also has its tragic movement. As it progresses, the apparent and submerged references to Christian grace and salvation, to religious typology and symbolism and myth—perceptively explicated by critic Harold P. Simonson— come increasingly to our attention, deepening our sense of the three characters—the narrator, the father, and the doomed brother Paul— and of the relationships between them.

In the second story, logger Jim Grierson spends his winters pimping and "rereading Jack London, omitting the dog stories" (122). In the last story, "USFS 1919: The Ranger, the Cook, and a Hole in the Sky," the allusions are more frequent, including a quotation from Matthew Arnold which opens and closes the story, and to which I wish to return later. Elsewhere in this story reference is made to Dante's *Inferno*, to a prostitute who spoke blank verse, to the prize-winning sonnet which Maclean wrote as a high school student "On Milton's Blindness," or rather which his mother wrote with her right hand while he held her trembling left hand, to his further efforts at scanning Milton and Shakespeare under his mother's tutelage.

Pursuing the references to spoken rhythm in "USFS 1919," it is worth noting that Maclean has written recently of the importance of students' understanding the rhythm of poems, and of teaching to college students, including even graduate students often ignorant of such matters, the rhythms of such apparently simple ballads as "Lord Randal" ("The Pure and the Good," 4). Thus Maclean's interest in speech rhythm in his stories may be credited to more than a naturally good ear, although his ear is very good indeed. Rhythms of various kinds underlie all of the book: the four-count rhythm of fly-casting, learned on a metronome, or to his father's clapping out a four-count rhythm with his hands, the rhythm of downward moving water in a mountain river, with its three-part pattern of rapids, deep pools, and shallowing tail-outs, before the pattern repeats itself. That rhythm, Maclean writes, reminds us that

> . . . stories of life are often more like rivers than books. But I knew a story had begun, perhaps long ago near the sound of water. And I sensed that ahead I would meet something that would never erode so there would be a sharp turn, deep circles, a deposit, and quietness. (63)

There is the rhythm of geologic time, of the succession of stages in the earth's history which is described in the title story and in "USFS 1919," where Blodgett Canyon's glacial record, written in stupendous mountain forms, seems to overwhelm the boy on his marathon hike, walking to the rhythm of " 'It's time to quit. It's time to quit' "(158). And again underlying this entire story there is the rhythm of the epic boyhood summer, ending with Quitting Time and Cleaning Out the Town. In the logging story, there is the rhythm of two-man crosscut sawing, the participants "lost in abstractions of motion and power. But when sawing isn't rhythmical, even for a short time, it becomes a kind of mental illness— maybe even something more deeply disturbing than that. It is as if your heart isn't working right"(113).

Maclean shows a liking for rhythmic triads in two of his three story titles, "Logging and Pimping and 'Your Pal, Jim,' " and "USFS 1919: The Ranger, the Cook, and a Hole in the Sky," triads which actually scan. And there are Maclean's beautiful parallel syntactic structures when the balanced and controlled effects of series consisting of two or three elements are spun out into hypnotic chains of four or five, with each element in the series held fixed and memorable by the polysyndeton of the repeated "ands": "Then in the Arctic half-light of the canyon, all existence fades to a being with my soul and memories and the sounds of the Big Blackfoot River and a four-count rhythm and the hope that a fish will rise"(104). At their best, as in the Blodgett Canyon scene in "USFS 1919" and at the end of the title story where the Biblical allusions

are echoed in Maclean's own verbal patterns, the author's rhythms
of rock and river and the human presence and the grace or art are
beautifully interrelated within a prose of sonorous power:

> Eventually, all things merge into one and a river runs
> through it. The river was cut by the world's great flood
> and runs over rocks from the basement of time. On some
> of the rocks are timeless raindrops. Under the rocks are
> the words, and some of the words are theirs.
> I am haunted by waters. (104)

The literary scholar's interest in the profound differences between
life and literature, between a mere record of events and a meaning-
ful shaping of these events into art, informs both the title story and
"USFS 1919." "What I remember most about my life is its literature," Maclean has said in describing his own reaction and that
of young readers to his book ("The Pure and the Good," 4–5).
Writing of King Lear in an essay published 35 years ago, Maclean
had noted this same distinction, and had similarly probed the sources
of art's appeal:

> . . . the world that is each poem is bound together so
> that it binds the hearts of those who look upon it, of whom
> the poet is one. To look upon a poem, then, as distinct
> from looking upon much of the succession of life, is to be
> moved, and moved by emotions that, on the whole, attract
> us to it and are psychologically compatible ("Episode,
> Scene, Speech, and Word," 597).

The wonder which accompanies the transformation of life into
literature is a central theme of "USFS 1919" and Maclean sets
forth its essence early in the story:

> I had as yet no notion that life every now and then be-
> comes literature—not for long, of course, but long enough
> to be what we best remember, and often enough so that

what we eventually come to mean by life are those moments when life, instead of going sideways, backwards, forward, or nowhere at all, lines out straight, tense and inevitable, with a complication, climax, and given some luck, a purgation, as if life had been made and not happened. (127)

The allusion to Aristotle here brings us closer to Maclean's scholarly touchstones. Without making too much of the concept of the "Chicago school" of literary criticism, and recognizing the plurality of critical approaches of the University of Chicago English faculty during Maclean's years there, it is still worth noting that Maclean's book reveals a close adherence to what might be considered the Chicago group's Neo-Aristotelian precepts. Among those tenets which seem most relevant to an understanding of *A River Runs Through It and Other Stories* are the beliefs that poetry, written large as literature, is more philosophical than history, that poetry or art thus seeks and expresses inevitable wholes, and that criticism inquires into the various parts by which these wholes achieve unity. Further, that the criticism of literature, in R. S. Crane's words, ought "to play a more influential role in the culture and action of the contemporary world," and that criticism must be seen as part of the range of humane studies, whose ideal "is the fullest possible discovery, in every subject matter, of its varied humanistic aspects" (2, 3).

Two of Norman Maclean's essays are included by Crane in his important manifesto of the Chicago Neo-Aristotelians, *Critics and Criticism: Ancient and Modern*, published in 1952. One of the Maclean pieces, on *King Lear*, cited earlier, is closely Neo-Aristotelian in its part-whole treatment of the play. The other, a much longer and more wide-ranging essay, represents the field of Maclean's principal scholarship, the theory of lyric poetry between the Renaissance and the Romantic age. Within this full and rewarding essay, "From Action to Image: Theories of the Lyric in the Eighteenth Century," may be found several important literary and aesthetic ideas which seem to me to inform the stories of *A River Runs Through It*.

"From Action to Image" describes and analyzes the effect upon
the writers and critics of the late seventeenth and eighteenth centuries of the rediscovery of the ancient Greek philosopher-critic Di-
onysius Longinus' treatise, *On the Sublime*. To summarize Maclean's
argument briefly, the reappearance of Longinus' essay had a major
effect upon lyric poetry and literary theory in the late seventeenth
and eighteenth centuries. Longinus brought the attention of contemporary scholars and writers to the qualities of literature which
" 'transport' the reader out of his normal senses and invest literary
works with immortality" (413). Although he does not stress the
sources of the sublime in the natural world (as do many of his fol-
lowers), Longinus does cite the presence of sublime natural objects
as evidence of a creator whose intentions for men are made clear in
these natural features. Like Maclean's own minister father, whose
favorite catechism—"Man's chief end is to glorify God, and to enjoy Him forever" (1) justifies his sense of joy in God's natural world,
Longinus conveys the belief that the creator inspires us to search in
the wonders of creation for the beauty which renders it delightful
(451).

Later in the eighteenth century, under the influence of critics like
Edmund Burke, a second term, beauty, is added to the sublime to
account for the entire aesthetic experience. Natural objects were
sublime or they were beautiful. The sublime—the massive, the elevated, the awesome in the natural world—moved the beholder toward emotional feelings of turbulence and transport. The beautiful
aroused the opposite effects of love and pity and sympathy for one's
fellow human beings, and of an emotional state of relaxation. The
concept of the beautiful, for the eighteenth century, was the lesser
of the two responses, and came to be associated, according to Maclean, with the lesser lyric poem. The higher part of the aesthetic
response was accorded to the sublime, whose associations were with
the more powerful emotions of fear and self-preservation, and which
came to be identified with the higher lyric form, the Great Odes of
the century.

In scholar Maclean's examination of how "this 'non-lyrical' age
regarded the highest form of the lyric—the Great Ode—as one of

(its) supreme expressions,'' we may find suggestive connections to artist Maclean's fictions (408). Writing in another non-lyrical age, Maclean also reaches toward sublimity, but in a contemporary laconic western American voice which must eschew not only the overt concept of sublimity—elevation, nobility, grandeur, solemnity, awe—but also the word itself and all its synonyms. Maclean nevertheless intimates the presence of sublimity in his stories through the lesser but more available concept of *beauty*.

The word "beautiful" rings like a ballad's refrain through the book, particularly in the title story and in "USFS 1919," those stories in which sublimity is felt as an unstated force. It is his father's word, we are told. "Unlike many Presbyterians, he often used the word 'beautiful' '' (10). Something of an eighteenth-century figure himself, with his stylish casting, his gloved casting hand, and his metronomical regularities of religion and fly-fishing, the elder Maclean serves to revivify for the sake of the stories the eighteenth-century belief that the beauties of the earth "were God's manifestation of his attributes and the lesser glories of man" ("From Action to Image," 445). Maclean says of his father, "He was about the only man I knew who used the word 'beautiful' as a natural form of speech, and I guess I picked up the habit from hanging around him when I was little" (95).

So the father's word becomes the son's, and in turn the scholar's and the writer's, each stage adding its own accretion of meaning. The Big Blackfoot where they fish is "a beautiful stretch of water" (16). Making an ash-soft cast, dropping the fly softly to the water is like "becoming the author of something beautiful" (43). The tragic brother Paul was "beautiful," both father and son concur (103). The memorable "USFS 1919" has this as its first sentence: "I was young and I thought I was tough and I knew it was beautiful and I was a little bit crazy but hadn't noticed it yet" (125). Even unpacking horses who have been loaded by a master is

> . . . beautiful—one wet satin back after another without
> saddle or saddle sore. . . . Perhaps one has to know about
> keeping packs balanced on the backs of animals to think

this beautiful, or to notice it at all, but to all those who work come moments of beauty unseen by the rest of the world.

So, to a horseman who has to start looking for horses before daybreak, nothing is so beautiful in darkness as the sound of a bell mare. (131)

The wonder and terror of life are in these stories: in the title story, Paul, swimming the turbulent and dangerous river with his rod in his right hand, reaching the rock in the middle, to which he clings precariously with his free left hand, then rising, streaming water, to begin his magnificent casting, the spray from which "enclosed him in a halo of himself" (20). Later, Paul moving into the river canyon's subterranean shadows, presaging the early death which will claim him. The river and the rocks beneath it, with raindrops on them, and beneath the rocks the words. The enormous ages of the earth. Masses of time to match masses of space. While it will not do for the author to say it, the sublime is present in all of this.

"USFS 1919" also stirs something of awe within us. As a fire lookout on a mountain top, the boy learns that it doesn't take much body or mind to be a lookout:

It's mostly soul. It is surprising how much our souls are alike, at least in the presence of mountains. For all of us, mountains turn into images after a short time, and the images turn true. Gold-tossed waves change into the purple backs of monsters, and so forth. Always something out of the moving deep, and nearly always oceanic. Never a lake, never the sky (144).

Lines from Matthew Arnold's "The Buried Life" begin and end this story, and their summoning of "the hills where his life rose" reinforces, with Arnoldian high seriousness, the sublimity of great mountains, and of the oceanic, the moving deep to which that life flows, and of the hole in the sky which the boy turned man and writer must invest with meaning.

Willa Cather claimed early in the 1920's that the thing not present on the page might be the most powerful presence there, that stories could be stronger for what they did not overtly state (41-43, 102-3). It was an idea that she proved again and again in her great understated works like *A Lost Lady*, *The Professor's House*, and *Death Comes for the Archbishop*. Young Ernest Hemingway was working along the same lines toward his "iceberg theory" that you could omit, if you knew that you omitted, and the omission would cause readers to feel more than they understood (*A Moveable Feast*, 75). "The dignity of movement of an iceberg," he said, "is due to only one-eighth of it being above water" (*Death in the Afternoon*, 192).

Something of that same dignity—perhaps only another name for sublimity—is present through our sense of its being withheld in stories like "USFS 1919" and "A River Runs Through It." In their way, they may be seen as exemplifying the classical unification of fear and pity, the sublime and the beautiful, which exist side by side in Aristotle and Longinus, but which a later age had seen fit to separate. In Maclean's best stories, they come together again, as lyric and ode, under the appellation of the beautiful, but bearing the force of the sublime.

WORKS CITED

Cawelti, John. Rev. of *A River Runs Through It and Other Stories*, by Norman Maclean. *The New Republic*, 1 May 1976: 24-26.

Cather, Willa. *On Writing*. New York: Alfred A. Knopf, 1949.

Crane, R. S. "Introduction." *Critics and Criticism: Ancient and Modern*. Chicago: University of Chicago Press, 1952. 1-24.

Hemingway, Ernest. *Death in the Afternoon*. New York: Charles Scribner's Sons, 1932.

Hemingway, Ernest. *A Moveable Feast*. New York: Charles Scribner's Sons, 1964.

Maclean, Norman. "Episode, Scene, Speech, and Word: The Madness of Lear." *Critics and Criticism: Ancient and Modern*. Ed. R. S. Crane. Chicago: University of Chicago Press, 1952. 595-615.

Maclean, Norman. "From Action to Image: Theories of the Lyric in the Eighteenth Century.'' *Critics and Criticism: Ancient and Modern*. Ed. R. S. Crane. Chicago: University of Chicago Press, 1952. 408–62.

Maclean, Norman. ''The Pure and the Good: On Baseball and Backpacking.'' *Association of Departments of English Bulletin* 61 (May 1979). 3–5.

Maclean, Norman. *A River Runs Through It and Other Stories*. Chicago: University of Chicago Press, 1976.

Simonson, Harold P. ''Norman Maclean's Two-Hearted River.'' *Western American Literature*. 17 (August 1982). 149–55.

Style and Grace

Wendell Berry*

Works of art participate in our lives; we are not just distant observers of *their* lives. They are in conversation among themselves and with us. This is a part of the description of human life;
we do the way we do partly because of things that have been said
to us by works of art, and because of things that we have said in
reply.

For a long time, I have been in conversation with "Big Two-
Hearted River," and with myself *about* "Big Two-Hearted River."
I have read the story many times, always with affection and gratitude, noticing and naming its virtues, and always seeing clearly in
imagination the landscape and all the events of Nick Adams' re-
storative fishing trip. It is this clarity with which Hemingway speaks
his story into the reader's imagination that is his great and char-
acterizing virtue:

The river made no sound. It was too fast and smooth. . . .
Nick looked down the river at the trout rising. . . . As far

*This essay was written especially for this volume and appears here for the first time
with the permission of the author.

down the long stretch as he could see, the trout were rising,
making circles all down the surface of the water, as though
it were starting to rain.

There is a moving courage in this plainness, freeing details, refusing
clutter.

But that is not what my conversation with this story has been
about. It has been about the ending, when Nick has fished down
the river to where it leaves the sunlight and enters a heavily wooded
swamp. At that point Nick turns back because "in the fast deep
water, in the half light, the fishing would be tragic."

The story ends: "There were plenty of days coming when he
could fish the swamp." I assume that such days were indeed coming, but they do not come in this story. And I have asked myself
what it means that the story ends where it does, and what Hemingway meant by "tragic."

So far, I have been unable to believe that he meant the word
literally. The swamp seems to be a place where one might hook big
fish and then lose them. But tragedy is not a name for the loss of
fish. Or it may be that Nick fears that fishing in the swamp would
make him sad, a dark swamp inevitably suggesting or symbolizing
what is mysterious or bewildering. But the correct name for such
sadness (in anticipation, at least) is melancholy, not tragedy. It is
hard to escape the feeling that Hemingway uses "tragic" more seriously than a casual speaker would use "awful" or "terrible," but
not much more. If he means the word seriously, then he is talking
about a tragedy that he knows about but the reader does not.

At any rate, the story receives a challenge at the end that it does
not accept. It refuses to go into the dark swamp. I think that what
it calls "tragic" is really messiness or unclarity, and that it refuses
out of a craftsmanly fastidiousness; it will not relinquish the clarity
of its realization of the light and the river and the open-water fishing. It is a fine story, on its terms, but its terms are straitly limited.

Similarly, the burned town and countryside at the beginning
might have been felt as tragic, suggestive as they are of the war-
damage in Nick's past—but they are felt, in fact, only as a kind of

cleansing away of all that is past, leaving Nick in isolation: "He felt he had left everything behind." That sentence sets the story in its bounds: it cannot be tragic because it is about a solitary man in an unmemoried time. So far as we can learn from the story itself, the man comes from nowhere, knows and is known by nobody, and is going nowhere—nowhere, at least, that he cannot see in full daylight.

"Big Two-Hearted River" seems to me, then, to be a triumph of style in its pure or purifying sense: the ability to isolate those parts of experience of which one can confidently take charge. It does not go into dark swamps because it does not know how it will act when it gets there. The problem with style of this kind is that it is severely reductive of both humanity and nature: the fisherman is divided from history and bewilderment, the river from its darkness. Like the similarly reductive technical and professional specializations of our time, this style minimizes to avoid mystery. It deals with what it does not understand by leaving it out.

Lately, my conversation with "Big Two-Hearted River" has been joined and a good deal clarified by Norman Maclean's long story, "A River Runs Through It," also a story about fishing, not so neat or self-contained as Hemingway's, but just as fine, on its own terms, and far more moving.

Fishing, in Mr. Maclean's story, is not a rite of solitary purification, a leaving of everything behind, but a rite of companionship. It is a tragic rite because of our inevitable failure to understand each other; and it is a triumphant rite because we can love completely without understanding. Fishing, here, is understood as an art, and as such it is emblematic of all that makes us companions with one another, joins us to nature, and joins the generations together. This is the connective power of culture; sometimes it works, sometimes it fails; when it fails, it fails into tragedy, but here it is a tragedy that confirms the completeness, and indeed the immortality, of love.

Though the river of "A River Runs Through It" is the Big Blackfoot which, so far as we are told, enters no swamp, the whole story takes place in a dark swamp of sorts: the unresolvable bewilderment of human conflict and affection and loss. The style is confident enough, for Mr. Maclean accepts fully the storyteller's need to speak wholeheartedly however partial his understanding, but it is not pure or self-protective. It is a style vulnerable to bewilderment, mystery, and tragedy—and a style, therefore, that is open to grace.

This story is profoundly and elatedly religious—though it is untainted by the doctrinal arrogance and the witless piety that often taint "religion." Reading it, we are not allowed to forget that we are dealing with immortal principles and affections, and with the lives of immortal souls. "In our family," the first sentence reads, "there was no clear line between religion and fly fishing." And one is inclined at first to take that as a little family joke. The sentence states, however, the author's conviction of the doubleness, the essential mysteriousness, of our experience, which presides over the story to the end, and gives it imaginative force of the highest kind.

The theme of fly fishing and (or as) religion is developed masterfully and with exuberant humor in the first few pages, which give the story its terms and its characters, its settled fate and its redemption. These pages sketch out the apprenticeship served by the writer and his younger brother, Paul, to their father, who was a Presbyterian minister and a fly fisherman:

> As a Scot and a Presbyterian, my father believed that man by nature was a mess and had fallen from an original state of grace. . . . I never knew whether he believed God was a mathematician but he certainly believed God could count and that only by picking up God's rhythms were we able to regain power and beauty.

"Our father's art" of fly fishing is seen, then, as a way of recovering God's rhythms and attaining grace—no easy task for "if you have never picked up a fly rod before, you will soon find it factually and theologically true that man by nature is a damn mess." Before he is "redeemed," "it is natural for man to try to attain power without recovering grace." These are sentences that we celebrate, reading them, because they are themselves celebrations of their own exact insight. "Power comes not from power everywhere, but from knowing where to put it on." The boys' father believed that "all good things . . . come by grace and grace comes by art and art does not come easy."

By the end of page six, not only have these connections been made between fishing and religion, art and grace, but our attention has been brought to focus on Paul, the brother, and we know that Paul is a superb fly fisherman and a compulsive gambler. By the end of page eight, we know also that he has a high temper, that he is inflexibly self-ruled, and that he is a street fighter. The story by then has its direction, which is as unbending as Paul's character. It is a story of the relentlessness of tragedy, and it is told with the relentlessness of the grace that comes by art. The story is relentlessly painful, and it relentlessly causes one to read on rejoicing to the end.

This is tragedy pretty much in the old Greek sense: a story of calamity and loss, which arrive implacably, which one sees coming and cannot prevent. But the relentlessness of the tragedy is redeemed by the persistence of grace. The entrances of grace come at moments of connection of man and fish and river and light and word and human love and divine love. If we see Paul drunk, defeated, jailed, and finally beaten to death, we also see him in glory. In the passage which follows the writer has sat down to watch his brother fish. Paul has swum out through dangerous water to a rock and climbed up on it and begun casting. There is no minimizing here:

> Below him was the multitudinous river, and, where the rock had parted it around him, big-grained vapor rose. The mini-molecules of water left in the wake of his line made momentary loops of gossamer. . . . The spray emanating from him was finer-grained still and enclosed him in a halo of himself. The halo of himself was always there and always disappearing, as if he were candlelight flickering about three inches from himself. The images of himself

and his line kept disappearing into the rising vapors of the river, which continually circled to the tops of the cliffs where, after becoming a wreath in the wind, they became rays of the sun.

The story is not in that, of course; that is only a glimpse that the story affords of the truest identity of the man it is about. The story is about the failure of the man to live up to his own grace, his own beauty and power, about the father's failure to be able to help, and about the writer's failure as his brother's keeper. And yet it is this glimpse and others like it that give the tragedy and the story their redemption and make possible the painful and triumphant affirmation at the end. This Paul, who failed, was yet a man who had learned the art of participating in grace. After his death, his brother and his father spoke of him, acknowledging their failure to help and to understand. The father asked:

> "Are you sure you have told me everything you know about his death?" . . . . I said, "Everything." "It's not much, is it?" "No," I replied, "but you can love completely without complete understanding." "That I have known and preached," my father said. . . .
>
> "I've said I've told you all I know. If you push me far enough, all I really know is that he was a fine fisherman."
>
> "You know more than that," my father said. "He was beautiful."

This story's fierce triumph of grace over tragedy is possible, the story "springs and sings," because of what I earlier called its vulnerability. Another way of saying this is that it does not achieve, because it does not attempt, literary purity. Nor does one feel, as one reads, that Mr. Maclean is telling the story out of literary ambition; he tells it, rather, because he takes an unutterable joy in telling it and therefore *has* to tell it. The story admits grace because it admits mystery. It admits mystery by admitting the artistically unaccountable. It could not have been written if it had demanded to consist only of what was understood or understandable, or what was entirely comprehensible in its terms. "Something within fishermen," the writer admits, "tries to making fishing into a world perfect and apart. . . ." But this story refuses that sort of perfection. It never forgets that it is a fragment of a larger pattern that it does not contain. It never forgets that it occurs in the world and in love.

I will not, I hope, be taken to be downgrading the literary art or literary value. This story is the work of a writer who has mastered his art, and I am fully aware that it would not be appreciable otherwise. I am only trying to make a distinction between two literary attitudes and their manifestation in styles.

Hemingway's art, in "Big Two-Hearted River," seems to me an art very considerably determined by its style. This style, like a victorious general, imposes its terms on its subject. We are meant always to be conscious of the art, and to be conscious of it as a feat of style.

Mr. Maclean's, on the other hand, seems to me a used, rather than an exhibited, art, one that ultimately subjects itself to its subject. It is an art not like that of the bullfighter, which is public, all to be observed, but instead is modest, solitary, somewhat secretive, used, like fishing, to catch what cannot be seen.

Norman Maclean: Selected Bibliography

Ron McFarland

WRITING BY MACLEAN:

" 'Billiards Is a Good Game': Gamesmanship and America's First Nobel Prize Scientist," *University of Chicago Magazine*, 67 (Summer 1975), 18–23. Maclean's memories of physicist Albert Michelson at the University of Chicago in 1928.

"Episode, Scene, Speech, and Word: The Madness of Lear," in *Critics and Criticism*, ed. Ronald S. Crane (Chicago: University of Chicago Press, 1952), 595–615. A work of criticism (only five footnotes), this essay on Shakespeare's tragedy is still highly regarded by many Shakespeare specialists.

"Exile on Grave Peak," *University of Chicago Magazine*, 68 (Spring 1976), 14–19. An excerpt from *A River Runs Through It and Other Stories*.

"From Action to Image: Theories of the Lyric in the Eighteenth Century," in *Critics and Criticism*, 408–460. This is an elaborate scholarly monograph (147 footnotes) concentrating on the ode as an example of 18th-century lyric theory.

"Generations: First and Second," in *American Dreams*, ed. Studs Terkel (New York: Pantheon, 1980), 112–14. An autobiographical piece mostly pertaining to Maclean's father.

"The Hidden Art of a Good Story: Wallace Stegner Lecture," at Lewis Clark State College in Lewiston, Idaho (May 1987). Observations on his own writing process. Printed here for the first time.

"A Man I Met in Mann Gulch," Talk at the Intermountain Fire Research Council in Missoula, Montana (31 October 1979). Concerns Harry Gisborne, Forest Service expert on fire management and the man in charge during the Mann Gulch fire of 1949, subject of Maclean's work in progress. Printed here for the first time.

"Montana Memory," Talk at the Institute of the Rockies in Billings, Montana (4 April 1977). Examines the tradition of story telling in Montana as a branch of frontier story telling in America. Uses the example of Charley Russell's stories. Printed here for the first time.

"The Pure and the Good: On Baseball and Backpacking," *Association of Departments of English Bulletin*, 61 (May 1979), 3–5. An essay on the craft of teaching and on the relationship between craft and art (specifically poetry).

"Retrievers Good and Bad," *Esquire*, 88 (October 1977), 22, 30, 32, 34, 36. A humorous, narrative essay on Maclean's experiences with his father and his first duck dogs.

A River Runs Through It and Other Stories. (Chicago: University of Chicago Press, 1976). Maclean's major work. Includes an essay of acknowledgements; the title novella; a short story, "Logging and Pimping and 'Your Pal, Jim' "; and a second novella, "USFS 1919: The Ranger, the Cook, and a Hole in the Sky."

———— Large Print Edition. (Boston: G. K. Hall, 1976).

———— Gift Edition. (Chicago: University of Chicago Press, 1983). Reissue of the title novella with fifteen color photographs, a new essay by Maclean, "On the Edge of Swirls," and a statement by photographer Joel Snyder.

"Teaching and Story Telling," Talk at the University of Chicago (19 February 1978), and at Montana State University in Bozeman, Montana (20 April 1978). General statement of the "poetics" underlying his own fiction, with specific applications to "A River Runs Through It." Printed here for the first time.

" 'This Quarter I Am Taking McKeon': A Few Remarks on the Art of Teaching," *University of Chicago Magazine*, 66 (January/ February 1974), 8–12. Originally presented as an address to the recipients of the Quantrell Award for Excellence in Undergraduate Teaching at the University of Chicago, this essay combines reminiscence, wit, and wisdom on the subject of teaching.

"The Woods, Books, and Truant Officers," *Chicago* (October 1977), 218–219, 248–251. An essay on how Maclean learned to write and why he continued, emphasizing his fascination with rhythm.

WRITINGS ABOUT MACLEAN:

Berry, Wendell. "Style and Grace." Printed here for the first time.

Blew, Mary. "Mo-nah-se-tah, the Whore, and the Three Scottish Women." Printed here for the first time.

Brittan, Jr. Gordon G. "Common Texts," *Montana State University Honors Lecture* (June 14, 1985), 1–6.

Dexter, Pete. "The Old Man and the River," *Esquire*, 95 (June 1981), 86–91.

Hesford, Walter. "Fishing for the Words of Life: Norman Maclean's 'A River Runs Through It,' " *Rocky Mountain Review of Language and Literature*, 34 (Winter 1980), 33–45.

Kittredge, William and Annick Smith. "The Two Worlds of Norman Maclean: Interviews in Montana and Chicago," *Tri-Quarterly*, 60 (Summer 1984), 412–432.

Love, Glen A. "On the Sublime and the Beautiful: Montana, Longinus, and Professor Norman Maclean." Printed here for the first time.

Nichols, Hugh, ed. "Art and Autobiography: An Interview with Norman Maclean." Unpublished.

O'Connell, Nicholas. "Norman Maclean," *At the Field's End: Interviews with Twenty Pacific Northwest Writers*, (Seattle: Madrona Publishers, 1987), 190–207.

Simonson, Harold P. "Norman Maclean's Two-Hearted River," *Western American Literature*, 17 (August 1982), 149–155.

Stegnes, Wallace. "Haunted by Waters." Printed here for the first time.

REVIEWS OF A RIVER RUNS THROUGH IT:

Signed reviews and feature articles.
Baker, James N. *Newsweek*, 88 (August 30, 1976), 70–71.
Breu, Giovanna. *People* (December 13, 1976), 90–92
Cawelti, John. *New Republic*, 174 (May 1, 1976), 24–26.
Frakes, James R. *New York Times Book Review* (September 19, 1976), 42.
Going, William A. *Book Forum*, 2 (Summer 1976), 454–456.
Keegan, Anne. *Chicago Tribune* (March 28, 1977).
Kotlowitz, Alex. *Wall Street Journal* (August 26, 1986).
Leopold, Wendy. *Los Angeles Times* (June 25, 1986).
Neill, Edward. *Times Literary Supplement* (January 14, 1977), 42.
Sale, Roger. *New York Review of Books*, 133 (May 27, 1976), 24.
Wild, Peter. *Western American Literature*, 19 (Winter 1985), 350–351.
Wimsatt, Margaret. *America*, 135 (October 2, 1976), 216–218.

Short reviews and notices.
AB Bookman's Weekly, 73 (January 23, 1984), 544.
Antioch Review, 35 (Spring 1977), 318.
Atlantic, 237 (June 1976), 105.
Booklist, 72 (June 15, 1976), 1451.
Book World (August 1, 1976), H10.
———— (June 3, 1979), E2.
Christian Science Monitor, 76 (December 13, 1983), 26.
Choice, 13 (September 1976), 826.
Commonweal, 111 (November 30, 1984), 662.
Kirkus Reviews, 44 (February 5, 1976), 216.
Kliatt Young Adult Paperback Guide, 13 (Fall 1979), 26.
New York Times, 133 (September 23, 1983), C21.
New York Times Book Review (April 15, 1979), 29.
Publishers Weekly, 209 (February 23, 1976), 117.
———— 215 (April 2, 1979), 72.
Saturday Review, 3ns (April 3, 1976), 32.
Sewanee Review, 85 (Winter 1977), ii.
Village Voice, 21 (March 29, 1976), 45.
———— 21 (May 17, 1976), 53.

Contributors

Wendell Berry farms and writes in Kentucky. Writer of ten collections of poetry and three novels, he is best known for his essays on farming life and the land. His most recent books are *Home Economics* (essays) and *Sabbath* (poems), both published in 1987.

Mary Clearman Blew writes fiction and teaches at Lewis Clark State College in Lewiston, Idaho. Her story, "Forby and the Mayan Maidens," is reprinted in *The Georgia Review: Fortieth Anniversary Fiction Retrospective* (Spring, 1986).

Gordon Brittan, Jr., teaches in the Department of Philosophy at Montana State University in Bozeman.

Pete Dexter, a columnist for the *Sacramento Bee*, has just seen the publication of his third novel, *Paris Trout*.

Walter Hesford directs the graduate and undergraduate programs in English at the University of Idaho in Moscow.

William Kittredge teaches fiction and essay writing at the University of Montana in Missoula. Author of two short story collections and several westerns, his most recent book is a collection of essays, *Owning It All* (1987).

Glen A. Love is Professor of English at the University of Oregon in Eugene. He is a frequent contributor to the scholarly journals on American literature. His most recent book is *New Americans: The Westerner & the Modern Experience in the American Novel* (1982).

Ronald E. McFarland teaches 17th-century and modern poetry at the University of Idaho. His most recent book is *The Villanelle: Evolution of a Poetic Form* (1987).

Hugh Nichols is Dean of the School of Arts and Sciences at Lewis Clark State College in Lewiston, Idaho, where he teaches courses in literature of the American West. He is editor of *Fiction Northwest*, forthcoming from Confluence Press (1989).

Harold Simonson is a professor of English at the University of Washington in Seattle. His most recent book is entitled *Prairies Within: The Tragic Triology of Ole Rolvaag* (1987).

Annick Smith lives in Missoula, Montana. She is best known for her work on the film, *Heartland* (1981).

Wallace Stegner has published over 20 works of fiction and nonfiction. His novel, *Angle of Repose*, won the Pulitzer Prize, and another novel, *Spectator Bird*, the National Book Award. *The American West as Living Space* and *Crossing to Safety* were both published in 1987.